Return B-w 7/19

NSWS

Please return/renew this item by the last date shown
on this label, or on your self-service receipt.

To renew this item, visit **www.librarieswest.org.uk**
or contact your library

Your borrower number and PIN are required.

Libraries**West**

OPEN WATER

BREAKING ICE

For Alicia, Camilla and Amelia

OPEN WATER
BREAKING ICE

THE POLAR OCEAN CHALLENGE
A VOYAGE OF EXPLORATION AROUND THE NORTH POLE

DAVID HEMPLEMAN-ADAMS

Sponsors

Without their kind support the expedition would not have been possible:

Artemis Fund Management Ltd

Medaire – Peter Tuggey Linda Porter

RDT – Graham Fever, Graham Murphy, Glen Taylor, Laughton Papworth

Mr Trotter's – Graham Jebb

Yuasa

Holt

Whale

The Bristol Port Company

PV Logic

Britannia Fire Ltd

St John Ambulance

Mamont Vodka

Mactra Marine Equipment

First published in Great Britain in 2017
Copyright © Cold Climate Expeditions Ltd and Simon Butler 2017

British Library Cataloguing-in-Publication Data
A CIP record for this title is available from the British Library

ISBN 978 0 85704 316 0

HALSGROVE
Halsgrove House,
Ryelands Business Park,
Bagley Road, Wellington, Somerset TA21 9PZ
Tel: 01823 653777   Fax: 01823 216796
email: sales@halsgrove.com

Part of the Halsgrove group of companies
Information on all Halsgrove titles is available at: www.halsgrove.com

Printed and bound in India by Parksons Graphics

Contents

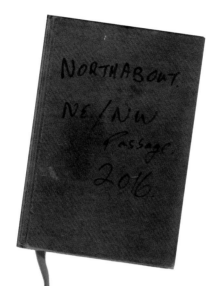

Battered but functional, my log book of the 2016 Ocean Challenge voyage – a short daily record of events aboard the Northabout.

Acknowledgements

I have to thank many people who have helped with making this book possible.

Steven Pugsley at Halsgrove Publishing, who has given encouragement and direction. My great thanks also to Simon Butler who took my ramblings and put them in some semblance of order and has become an expert on all things polar and sailing and I gained a new friend.

To the people who wash up behind my work to allow me to go off and do these mad adventures; in particular, Nicky and Sue.

The people and sponsors who have backed me in one way or another, without their help there wouldn't be any expeditions.

Dick Turpin, Frederik Paulsen, Mark Tyndall, Sir Malcolm Walker, Peter Cruddas, Richard Matthewman, Norman Stoller, Lord Kirkham, Peter Buckley.

And to all my friends and colleagues of the crew who have sweated, shivered, and lost sleep on so many watches; too many to name. You know who you are. Thank you.

To Jarlath Cunnane who built the magnificent *Northabout*.

Special thanks must go to Cheryl Lingard, Nick, Colin Walker, Clive Bailey and Frances Gard who kept the project on track.

All the lads at Sharpness who worked long hours to get the boat ready.

Special thanks to all the brilliant members at Thornbury Yacht Club for all of their help and support.

Steve and Ros Edwards for their continued support and friendship that helped to make this expedition and book possible. For adventures past and dreams to come.

OTHER BOOKS BY DAVID HEMPLEMAN-ADAMS

A Race Against Time
Toughing It Out
Walking on Thin Ice
At the Mercy of the Winds
Heart of the Great Alone
No Such Thing As Failure

Foreword

To sail the North East and North West Passages has been the dream of explorers and adventurers for centuries. Inspired by the exploits of such men, among them my Norwegian countrymen, Fridtof Nansen and Roald Amundsen, I was able to follow in their wake when, in 2010, I circumnavigated the North Pole along with Thorleif Thorleifsson in our little boat *Northern Passage*, the first to sail around the Arctic through both the North East and North West Passage in a single season. Whereas for centuries expeditions to the region had faced impassable ice, our voyage helped open the world's eyes to the effects of global warming on the rapidly diminishing arctic ice.

In the early planning stages of my expedition I had sought out my fellow adventurer David Hempleman-Adams as a man I knew who would relish the idea of such an undertaking. Sadly, David was committed to other enterprises and was unable to join me, but it was naturally with great interest that I followed his progress when he embarked on his own attempt aboard *Northabout* in 2016.

As with my own book *Northern Passage*, I believe is vital that we record the details of such journeys, not only for future generations, but in order that the world is woken up to the effects that rapid climate change is having on these hitherto remote regions of the earth. I therefore congratulate David and his crew, for not only completing their hazardous voyage, but in creating this important and hugely entertaining record of their adventure.

Børge Ousland
Norway 2017

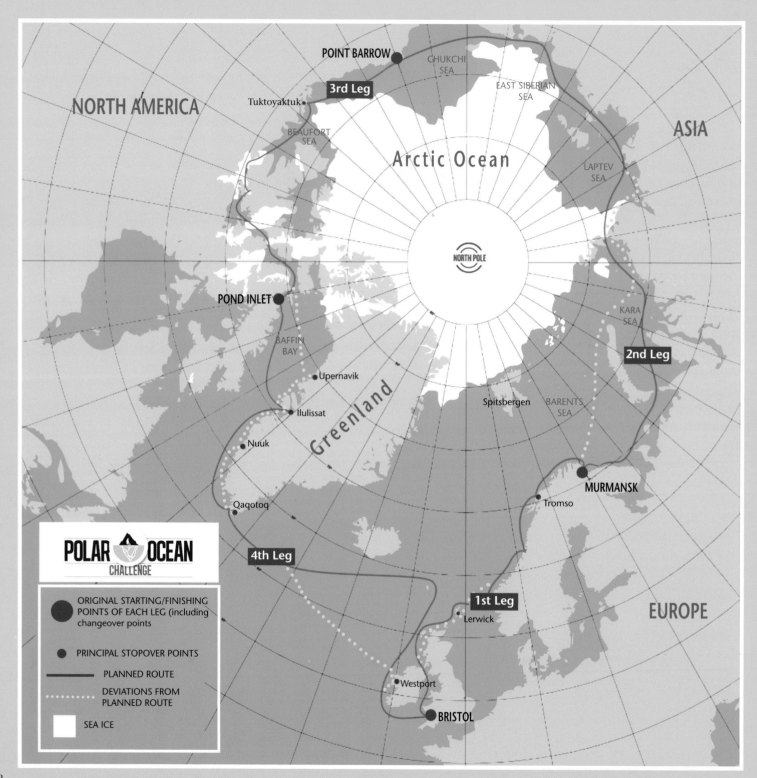

POINT BARROW

CHUKCHI SEA

EAST SIBERIAN SEA

3rd Leg

NORTH AMERICA

ASIA

Tuktoyaktuk

BEAUFORT SEA

Arctic Ocean

LAPTEV SEA

POND INLET

NORTH POLE

KARA SEA

BAFFIN BAY

Upernavik

2nd Leg

Spitsbergen

BARENTS SEA

Greenland

Ilulissat

Nuuk

MURMANSK

Qaqotoq

Tromso

4th Leg

1st Leg

EUROPE

Lerwick

POLAR OCEAN
CHALLENGE

ORIGINAL STARTING/FINISHING
POINTS OF EACH LEG (including
changeover points

Westport

PRINCIPAL STOPOVER POINTS

BRISTOL

PLANNED ROUTE

DEVIATIONS FROM
PLANNED ROUTE

SEA ICE

Preface

Time. *In the dim light of* Northabout's *cramped cabin I glance at my watch, the second-hand climbing slowly toward the hour mark. It is almost 2.00am – two hours into a four-hour watch and my fellow crew members are asleep. The boat rises under a sluggish swell and the rigging lines clatter impatiently against the mast.*

Time. *It's already a full week into August and we've been anchored, close to the most northern tip of Russia, for almost a week, arriving here full of expectation and excitement, only to be thwarted by the ice fields ahead. Nikolai, our Russian skipper, who has previously sailed both the North East and North West Passages, overwintering on each occasion, has warned against proceeding based on the information we've received from ice maps and reports from ice breakers. But I'm acutely aware, even against my own better judgement, that time is running out. Unless we move soon, our chances of making it around the Pole in one summer season is diminishing by the hour.*

The author.

Time. *On no other expedition, whether climbing Mount Everest or on my lone treks across the polar ice cap, has time played quite so much on my mind. In direct conflict with the elements one seldom has the luxury of contemplation. Decision-making is immediate. Here, in the wee small hours, one has an uncomfortable amount of time to dwell on the problems ahead. And while all such endeavours are time-critical, here, perhaps because so many others are reliant upon my decision-making, and conscious of the financial cost should we fail, the pressure is more acute. I am reluctant to challenge Nikolai's experience but I'm also aware of the signs of the crew becoming tetchy – looking to me for decisions. Choices that can mean success or failure, even life or death, for us all.*

Time. *I sense* Northabout *swinging her bow towards the north as the wind freshens. Perhaps tomorrow the ice fields ahead will at last begin to break into open water.*

David Hempleman-Adams

Nineteenth-century artists were inspired by the heroic stories related by those who returned from remote parts of the world, interpreting the scenes on canvas from their imaginations. Here HMS Erebus *and* Terror *are depicted on Captain William Parry's search for the North West Passage, in the 1820s, tossed in ice-bound seas with mountainous peaks rising in the distance. The same two vessels later accompanied John Franklin on his ill-fated expedition.*

In the Wake of *Erebus* and *Terror*

Terra Incognita is the name engraved on early maps given to those regions on earth where no civilised man had yet trod. These regions were the undiscovered planets of their day and they drew early adventurers to them as moths to a flame. Names such as Christopher Columbus, Vasco da Gama and Ferdinand Magellan reverberate from history, as do heroic British seafarers, Drake, Raleigh and Hudson, among others, each helping cartographers to fill in the gaps on the shrinking world map.

In later centuries, driven by commercial demands of ever more powerful nations, even the most remote regions gave themselves up to conquest. Yet there remained one region, while offering the prospects of untold wealth and strategic dominance, that remained unconquerable. Bound in ice, the arctic seas surrounding the northern polar cap, seemed forever destined to remain an unknown realm.

Driven by those with vested interests in developing links with the New World, and, in particular finding a northern sea route between the Atlantic and Pacific Oceans, the British in particular were determined to establish if such a passage were possible. As is often the case, it was a disastrous outcome of one of these early expeditions that became emblazoned in British history as a tragic but heroic endeavour, and one which led to the secrets of the North West Passage ultimately becoming unlocked.

In 1845, Royal Navy officer Sir John Franklin, already an experienced, if somewhat unlucky, leader of expeditions in

Rear Admiral Sir John Franklin.

HMS Terror *icebound, from a drawing by Sir George Back made on his 1836 exploration of the northern end of Hudson Bay during which* Terror *remained fast in the ice for 10 months This is the same vessel that Franklin took on his 1845 expedition – a huge tribute to the strength of these ships, originally designed as bomb vessels. Our Northabout, though much smaller, was also built with tackling ice specifically in mind.*

11

A page from my personal Log of our voyage in Northabout *showing hastily drawn-up calculations of fuel use during the expedition, more of which in later chapters.*

Sir Robert McClure (1807–1873).

the Canadian far north, accepted the offer to lead a well-equipped expedition the prime objective of which was to chart 300 or so miles of the North West Passage that remained unexplored. Aged 59, Franklin was in command aboard HMS *Terror,* with James Fitzjames captaining the accompanying HMS *Erebus.*

Both vessels were equipped with steam engines, novel for the time, and designed to provide the ships with motive power beyond that of conventional sail, while also providing a distillation plant to produce fresh water and a primitive central heating system for the crew. Also new was the provision of large quantities of tinned foodstuffs (in all the expedition was supplied with enough material to survive for three years), on the face of it a boon, but due to poor preparation in the canning process the tins allowed lead to be leached into the contents.

I have some sympathy for those responsible for provisioning expeditions where much of the time is to be spent at sea. Unlike Franklin, who had the might of the Royal Navy victualling commissioners behind him, I was tasked with the over-all responsibility for stocking *Northabout* with enough food, water and fuel for each leg of our journey, taking into account the possibility that there must be sufficient supplies to see us through should the vessel become ice bound, as could easily happen despite the recent rapid shrinking of the ice fields.

Especially where the lives of others are at stake, expedition leaders can leave nothing to chance and, as Franklin and many others have found, even the most meticulous plans are subject to the unforeseen. The sad fate of Franklin and the crews of *Terror* and *Erebus* trapped in the ice for over two years and likely going mad from lead poisoning, is a tale gradually unfolding as the melting ice reveals more evidence of their demise.

Five years after Franklin had sailed from Greenhithe, The McClure Arctic Expedition set off, principally to attempt to discover the fate of Franklin and, in part, to further British knowledge of the region. Irishman Robert McClure, distant countryman to the builder of *Northabout,* was an experienced Arctic explorer having been both on Back's 1836 expedition and later sailing with James Clark Ross on one of the three expeditions sent off to look for Franklin. In his third and final voyage to the arctic, in 1850, McClure commanded HMS *Investigator,* which along with HMS *Enterprise,* sailed from England via the Strait of Magellan into the Pacific and thence into the Arctic Ocean by way of the Bering Strait. Ice bound, McClure left the *Investigator* and continued eastwards by sled and on foot, meeting up in 1853 with a British expedition sailing from the east, eventually returning to England. Thus the McClure expedition became the first to transit the North West Passage as well as the first to circumnavigate the Americas.

It was not until 1903 that the first successful seagoing transit was achieved by one of the greatest names in Arctic exploration, the Norwegian Roald Amundsen.

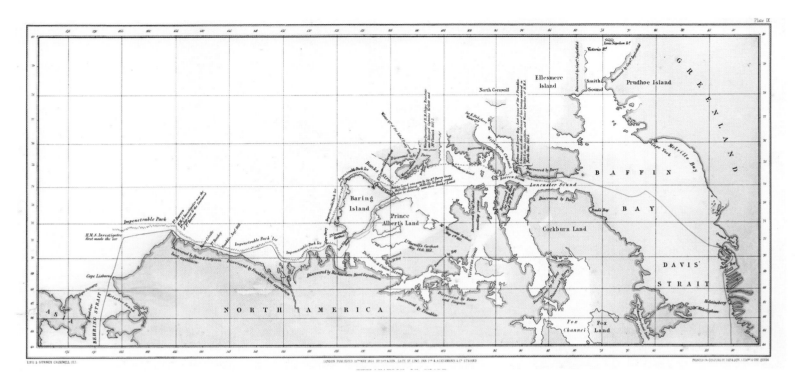

His exploits have done much to encourage myself and many others into a life of endeavour and adventure.

However, among my many non-British explorer friends, I am affectionately taken to task for our nation's ability to turn failures into heroic successes. For example why we give Robert Scott's ill-judged attempt to be the first to reach the South Pole more prominence in our history books than Amundsen's 1911 achievement. The fact is that men such as Amundsen and Fridjof Nansen had more direct experience of polar travel, learning from the peoples of the region how best to survive in extreme conditions.

Even today I much prefer to take on my own expeditions the same types of clothing and equipment that my Scandinavian contemporaries have tried and tested.

Contemporary map depicting the route of McClure's 1850 expedition showing the passage taken by HMS Investigator *(continuous red line) and the final transit of the North West Passage on foot (dotted red line) to where the party met up with HMS* Phoenix *sailing from the east. The chart was drawn by Samuel Gurney Cresswell, Second Lieutenant aboard the* Investigator *who led the party across the ice on its final leg and who is today credited with being the first person to traverse the North West Passage.*

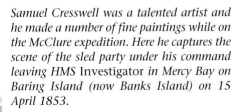

Samuel Cresswell was a talented artist and he made a number of fine paintings while on the McClure expedition. Here he captures the scene of the sled party under his command leaving HMS Investigator *in Mercy Bay on Baring Island (now Banks Island) on 15 April 1853.*

13

Inspired in part by the exploits of his countryman, Nansen, it was in 1903 that Amundsen and a crew of six, set off in the 45 ton fishing boat *Gjoa*, to complete their historic transit of the North West Passage, travelling via Baffin Bay to Nome in Alaska, overwintering for two successive seasons at King William Island.

Much like our own plans aboard *Northabout*, Amundsen had chosen a vessel with relatively shallow draft in which it was possible to sail close to land where in summer the ice was less of a danger to navigation.

*   *   *

Having achieved success in *Gjoa* and, in 1911, becoming the first to reach the South Pole, Amundsen turned his attention to the North East Passage, hoping to explore further into the ice fields north and east of Nansen's 1893 expedition in *Fram*. While Nansen's goal was to explore the possibility of reaching the North Pole by using the natural drift of polar ice, Amundsen, in *Maud*, was principally interested in entering the unknown regions of the Arctic Ocean.

These two Norwegians followed in the footsteps of early navigators who, from the fifteenth century, recognised the commercial advantages to be gained by opening a sea route between the northern Atlantic and Pacific Oceans. By the

Roald Amundsen (1872-1928) the first to transit the North West Passage by sea. Amundsen's boat Gjoa, *is now on display at the* Fram *Museum in Oslo.*

Largely driven by commercial interests, such of those of whaling companies, the waters off the northern coast of Russia grew in strategic importance from the seventeenth century onwards, not least as they promised a North East Passage between the Atlantic and Pacific Oceans. Abraham Storck's painting dated 1690 shows Dutch whalers off the coast of Spitsbergen.

seventeenth century regular coastal trade was underway between Archangel and the Yamal Peninsula, a route that was known as the Mangazeya seaway. In 1619, fearing the penetration of Western powers into Siberia, the Russians closed this seaway – the beginnings of a restrictive control over the route which continues to this day, as my experience in obtaining permits for the Polar Ocean Challenge expedition, described in later chapters, bears witness.

The first successful transit of the North East Passage is credited to a Portuguese explorer and trader, Daniel Melgueiro, who in 1660 (and in order to avoid pirates on the southern route), sailed from Japan into the Arctic Ocean via the Bering Strait. Reaching 84° North and siting the islands of Svalbard, he turned his vessel southward into the Atlantic, arriving in Porto in 1662.

Following in the footsteps of the early adventurers, Northabout *glides past the Svalbard islands on the calmest of seas. This was the island group that led the navigator Daniel Melgueiro into the Atlantic having made his historic transit of the North East Passage.*

15

Amundsen's Maud *trapped in ice. The intention of the expedition was to drift with the Polar ice towards the North Pole, but after surviving three winters in the grip of sea ice* Maud *entered open water and sailed on to Seattle.*

Melgueiro's voyage is particularly interesting to me in view of my own determination that the Polar Ocean Challenge and its associated charity, Wicked Weather Watch, should throw light on the consequences of Polar ice melt, for it is known that the years immediately preceding 1660 were the warmest in over two centuries. There's little doubt that Melgueiro chose this northern route in full knowledge that the route was, temporarily, ice free.

From the seventeenth century onwards adventurers such as Semyon Dezhnez, Vitus Bering, Alexsey Chirikov and Semyon Chelyuskin advanced our knowledge of the region, but it was not until 1878 that the Swedish *Vega* expedition made the successful crossing of the North East Passage from west to east, led by Adolf Erik Nordenskiöld.

Roald Amundsen was perhaps the last of the pioneers of exploration in the region. His expedition in *Maud*, which began on the eve of the Great War in July 1918, came as the development of powered flight gradually drew back the veil from the hitherto uncharted globe. In May 1926 Richard Byrd was claiming to be the first aviator to have crossed the North Pole in a fixed-wing aircraft, the same month in which *Norge*, a semi-rigid airship carried out the first verified overflight, an expedition also led by the remarkable Amundsen.

I have the greatest admiration for these early aviators, just as I do for those early explorers who attempted arctic journeys by boat. Indeed, my own record-breaking balloon flight to the North Pole in May 2000 was very much a tribute to the Swedish balloonist, Salomon Andrée, and his two colleagues whose ill-fated yet heroic attempt on the Pole in *Eagle,* in 1897, fired my imagination.

*　　*　　*

One thing is certain. Of all those who sailed with me in *Northabout* on the Polar Ocean Challenge, none underestimated the potential dangers of what lay ahead but carried with them the spirit of all those who went before. And perhaps we are among the last of those who will witness the region as a true wilderness.

A Life of Adventure

I am including this short chapter in order to help put the Polar Ocean Challenge expedition in to context. This voyage was quite different from many of my earlier endeavours which, I suppose, largely involved setting myself specific goals, often in solitary competition against the natural world, in order to achieve specific objectives.

It's difficult to say exactly what drives a person to put themselves at risk for the sake of, often indefinable, aims but one can only point to the lives of the earlier adventurers who were also impelled, in the words of the poet 'To strive, to seek, to find and not to yield'.

Mountains have always been my first love and I have fond schoolboy memories of trips to the Brecon Beacons, under the eye of our inspirational teacher Mansel James, sleeping in old army tents and exploring the countryside. Here I immediately felt a sense of belonging amid the magnificent isolation of the Welsh mountains. This was also the golden era of British climbers, with names such a Chris Bonington, Dougal Haston and Doug Scott ever present in the media.

Trips to the USA in my late teens allowed time to hone rock climbing skills and, in my early twenties, I had climbed many of the highest Alpine peaks including the Matterhorn, Mont Blanc and the Eiger. Then came Mount McKinley, North America's highest peak – a climb that could easily have cost the lives of myself and my climbing buddy Steve Vincent, an adventure which taught me valuable lessons for the future.

Steve Vincent (right) my climbing partner and myself, aged 18, on one of our climbing adventures in the USA.

On the summit of Everest, 2011.

"If you can meet with Triumph and Disaster
And treat those two impostors just the same."

Rudyard Kipling had it just about right, although at the time my 1983 failure (top) to reach the North Pole was a bitter pill to swallow. But, in 1996, made my arrival at the South Pole (centre) seem all the sweeter. As did my arrival (above) at the North Pole with Rune Gjeldnes in 1998.

Later came greater challenges in South America, Africa and eventually, literally the pinnacle, the Himalayas and Everest. In the course of my climbing career I've climbed the highest peaks on all seven continents but it may come as a surprise when I tell you that on first reaching the summit of Mount Everest, amid the exhaustion, relief and elation, I also felt strangely disappointed. Nor do I think I'm alone in experiencing this emotion – which perhaps confirms the motivation for the true adventurer comes not from the desire to achieve success but from the endeavour itself.

Of course I was gutted when my 1983 attempt to reach the North Pole ended with broken ribs and in failure, but few things are worth attaining where the possibility of failure is absent. And few environments are so challenging as are found at the polar extremities of our planet. Indeed, the following year, when I became the first person to walk solo and unsupported to the Magnetic North Pole my sense of achievement was all the greater because of that earlier disappointment.

Success or failure, these high mountains and the vast empty spaces of the polar regions never failed to bring back that sense of 'belonging' I first felt when treking in the Brecon Beacons many years before.

Then came flying. To me a whole new challenge, opening up a vast and exciting world of adventure and exploration. It could even be said that my unsuccessful second attempt, with Rune Gjeldnes, to reach the Geographic North Pole in 1997 led me to first start contemplating alternative and novel approaches to reaching that goal. And so ballooning came seriously into my life.

If at first you don't succeed – on my way to the Geographical North Pole with Rune Gjeldnes, and a triumph of being the first to complete the Explorers' Grand Slam – to reach both Poles and climb the highest peaks on all seven continents.

After some expert tuition, during which time I crammed in as much knowledge about the complex technical issues around modern ballooning as I could, I unwisely decided that my first significant solo flight should be to take a hot air balloon over the Andes, a feat otherwise unattempted (or avoided!) by anyone before. That I was successful was in some ways due to beginners' luck.

Around this time I became fascinated by the exploits of the Swedish aeronaut and explorer, Salomon Andrée, whose nineteenth-century life combined my own passion for polar exploration and my newfound love of ballooning. This led to my emulation of the 1897 attempt made by Andrée and his two brave companions, Nils Strinberg and Knut Frænkel, to reach the North Pole in a hydrogen balloon, *Eagle*. Though their exploits were made all the more heroic by the lack of a realistic chance of success, I was determined to keep as close to the true ballooning experience as possible, opting for a wicket basket slung beneath the canopy of *Britannic Challenger* rather than the enclosed capsule favoured by modern balloonists.

Thus it was that on 28 May 2000 I took off from Spitsbergen, flying successfully over the North Pole on 1 June, before returning, somewhat miraculously, to Spitsbergen three days later.

With the balloon bug now firmly embedded in my bloodstream the following years found me, among other things, unsuccessfully attempting two crossings of the Atlantic (2002–3), successfully breaking the airship speed, distance and altitude record (2004), breaking the world altitude record for a Rozier balloon (2004), and the same record in a hot air balloon (2007), also the year in which I finally crossed the Atlantic by balloon – very much a case of third time lucky!

As I stated at the start of this chapter, I briefly relate these various adventures only to provide a background to my involvement in the Polar Ocean Challenge, to show how my earlier experiences provided essential know-how in getting the Challenge off the ground, and also to illuminate what a different experience this expedition would be for me.

*   *   *

Asked where my drive for continuous adventure comes from, and it's difficult for me to say. You'll probably get a different answer from anyone you ask whose life has been spent on such endeavours. Like any young boy I enjoyed reading about the wider world, and magazines such as the *National Geographic* opened my eyes to how different things were elsewhere on our planet. I loved watching TV programmes too and fondly remember the series that Jacques Cousteau produced, creating a wonderful sense of adventure in seeking out new and different things.

Andrée and Frænkel survey the beached Eagle *as she lies stranded on the polar ice in July 1897. The tragedy of the expedition, underprepared and fraught with technical difficulties could have been avoided but for Andrée's misplaced optimism, driven by the huge public interest generated in the expedition. It was only thirty years after their disappearance that the remains of the party came to light, including Strinberg's intact photographic plates.*

Britannic Challenger *touches down at the end of my polar flight in June 2000.*

Expedition Leader? It's always a title that I've been wary of using.

One of the books I read at school, a story which has remained with me, was Heinrich Harrer's *The White Spider*, which described the first successful ascent of the Eiger's north face. A thrilling story so well told – and if you have the seeds of adventure in you, stories such as this nurture them.

For me, there was the brilliant teacher at my school, Mansel James, who organised the school's participation in the Duke of Edinburgh Awards. Being quite competitive and, even at 13, a self-reliant kid, this suited me down to the ground. I remember on one of our group expeditions in the Brecon Beacons we had to reach a particular checkpoint by 6.00pm but there was no way that was going to happen, so I set off by myself. When I arrived, well in time, and expecting to get some praise, Mansel James, with a look of real disappointment, asked where the rest of the party was. I remember even now his words 'Always bring back your dead.'

This lesson, that when working with a team, it's not about your own survival or personal achievements. Real success resides in achieving the goal together. For this reason, in relation to the Polar Ocean Challenge, I've always been ambivalent about being called 'Expedition Leader'. To be frank, my attitude is that if one of the party members were suddenly to say 'I'm not doing that' – then there's bugger-all one can do about it. And, while I've many hundred of hours sailing experience I do not call myself a sailor. Certainly having expended so much effort in securing the skippering services of Nikolai Litau, whose experience in arctic waters was second to none, what would be the point of not acceding to his judgement throughout the trip.

In the end, if I had a role of Expedition Leader at all on *Northabout*, bearing in mind also that I would not be participating in all four legs, my efforts were better spent creating a team in which all felt they had their part to play.

Myself and some of the crew aboard Northabout. *Achieving the goal together.*

The Polar Ocean Challenge

This was something different for me. No particular records to be broken, no personal challenges other than to see the job done. To prepare for a difficult voyage that, in its success, was as much for the satisfaction of others as it was for myself. This brought different pressures to its planning stages in which I was reliant on the help and experience of many others, although ultimately I knew that the buck stopped with me.

The Polar Ocean Challenge, for me, presented a more important opportunity than just adventure, for it gave an opportunity to show the world the dramatic effects of global warming. Effects that would bring vast changes, not only to human life on the planet, but threaten the survival of the animal and plant life that dependent upon this vast and fragile polar eco-system both on land and in the sea.

The seeds of the project were sown as a result of my first visits to the arctic over twenty-five years ago, and taking part in many expeditions since, I've witnessed the somewhat alarming changes in the region brought about by the retraction of sea ice. Over 13 per cent of the sea ice has disappeared and it has been established that the region is at its warmest for at least 40 000 years, the seasonal melt lengthening by five days per decade.

Aboard Northabout *poling our way through ice. Despite the retraction of polar ice, the success of the Polar Ocean Challenge was by no means a certainty and we were at the mercy of nature should the ice close in.*

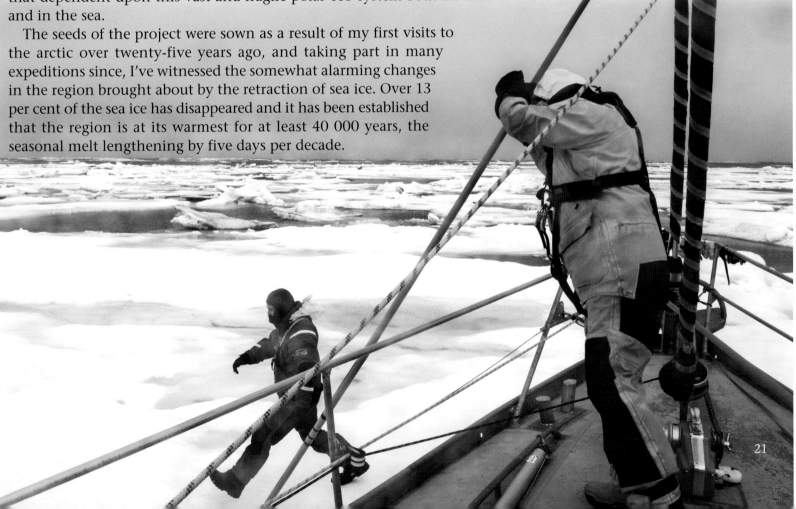

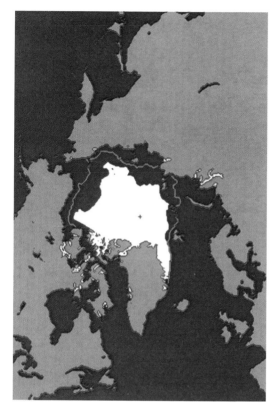

As well as the long term decline in the arctic ice, there are annual monthly fluctuations which determined the optimum dates for our departure and our choice of route. These two ice charts show the relative extent of the ice in March (left) and in November. On our voyage, timing was critical and by leaving Bristol in June 2016 we calculated our journey around the Pole to coincide with the depletion of ice as we progressed. As ever, the best laid plans...

Throughout the voyage we received detailed ice charts on a daily basis (included in later chapters) which allowed us to more carefully plan our route and to make decisions on whether it was possible for Northabout *to proceed.*

These dramatic environmental changes have opened up the seaways otherwise impassable or severely ice-restricted. Our aim was to spend the arctic summer sailing anti-clockwise around the world, circumnavigating the North Pole, in itself a 13 500 mile round trip, and with no guarantee of success. The route would take us through both the North East and North West Passages. A little more than a century ago the North East Passage might have taken two or three years to transit due to the extent of the ice, and the North West Passage was considered impassable until Amundsen's historic voyage in 1903. Even in more recent years each passage might take two or three seasons to transit dependent upon the extent of the sea ice.

Now, for the first time it was possible to realistically consider completing the voyage in a single year, although this was by no means certain. Even given the most favourable circumstances we would require luck, skillful navigation based on accurate weather and sea ice data, and expert knowledge and experience of sailing in these treacherous waters. It was my job to ensure the chances of becoming trapped in the ice were kept to a minimum, but also to have a contingency should that happen.

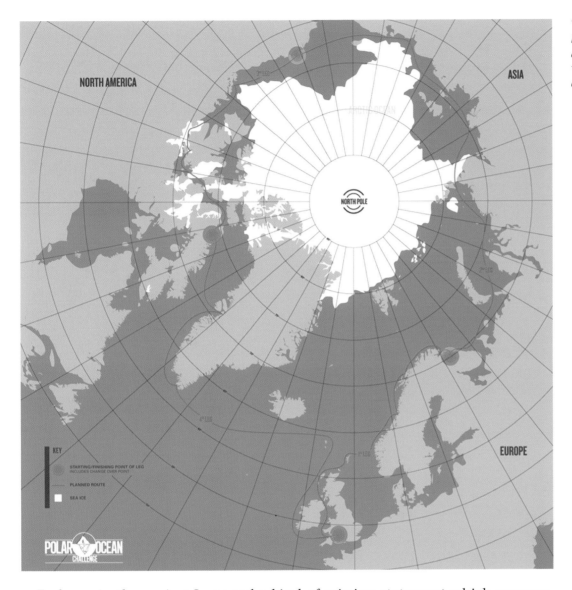

The Polar Ocean Challenge route to be taken by Northabout. *My original planned start date of 2015 being postponed for a year while we took* Northabout *on her shake down cruise.*

Early on in the project I penned a kind of mission statement which encapsulated my aims and ambitions for the Polar Ocean Challenge:

I see this possibility to circumnavigate the Arctic as one I wanted to take despite the risks associated with it in order to increase the worlds attention on the effects of Arctic climate change. There may be a possibility still to curb this progressive warming and melting in the Arctic. But even if this is not possible the next most important thing is to at the very least highlight the need to 'Navigate the Future of the Arctic responsibly'. Shipping will pass through very soon, the lives of people living in the

Børge Ousland's Corsair trimaran, Northern Passage, *in which he and Thorlief Thorleifsson became the first to complete the North East and North West Passages in a single year. This vessel was some 5 meters shorter that* Northabout *but with a crew of two rather than five or six.*

normally year round ice bound communities, well, their lives will change drastically. As are the habitats of walruses, whales, seals, polar bears, the whole ecosystems within the sea. We can try to have an impact in trying to make sure that this change is handled carefully, sustainably, responsibly. I believe that all of us, we can all be part of that conversation.

I have also set up a charity called Wicked Weather Watch which is an education based program which is engaging with schools on the issues of climate change notably in the Arctic area. This is because it is the polar regions that I am most familiar with and where it would appear, certainly in the Arctic that climate change is very noticeable. Non scientist people like myself who, because I have been travelling to the polar regions for over 30 years now, have been witness to those changes first hand and bring another perspective alongside the scientific observations.

*   *   *

I'd had a chance to take part in an earlier expedition led by the Norwegian explorer Børge Ousland, who in 2010, along with Thorleif Thorleifsson, became the first to complete the polar circumnavigation in a single summer in his trimaran *Northern Passage.* I'd first met Børge in Punta Arenas in the winter of 1995/6 when I was attempting to become the first Briton to reach the South Pole, solo and unsupported. Other plans made it impossible for me to accept the offer to join him on *Northern Passage* and I was determined not to let another opportunity pass.

In all my previous expeditions, experience had taught me valuable lessons in how far one must go in planning. While drawing up careful plans was a key element in success, it was not proof against failure. Indeed over-planning – that is attempting to cater for every eventuality – only increased one's anxiety before setting off and never solved unforeseen problems, which as the name suggests can't be planned against.

I believe instinct based on experience is a formidable tool for the explorer. For the Polar Ocean Challenge, however, I also had to cater for those who were to join the expedition and, as later chapters reveal, there were a hundred and one things that, at the outset, one never even thought about – and at this early point in the venture I didn't even have a boat!

Northabout

Life can sometimes appear to be just a series of coincidences and certainly the Polar Ocean Challenge would never have happened had I not fallen in with friends and fellow explorers at a point when the stars of fortune were colliding.

It was in 2010 that I travelled with Alicia, my eldest daughter, in order to meet up with my old friend, the renowned arctic adventurer, Frederik Paulsen, bound for a trip to Franz Josef Land on board an icebreaker. While stopping over in Murmansk I met up with Børge Ousland again. He was aboard *Northern Passage* waiting for his permits from the Russians so that he might proceed on his polar voyage. Poor Børge was tearing his hair out in frustration – every hour the permit delays making his chances of success ever more remote.

Only later did I come to appreciate quite how critical were these permits for any expedition attempting a voyage through Russian waters. Now, witnessing Børge's furious frustration, provided a valuable lesson in planning my own journey years later. As we sat in the cramped cockpit of *Northern Passage* I marvelled at Børge's intrepid sense of adventure, setting off in what appeared to be little more than a tent perched above heavily-laden canoes floating beneath a single mast. Yet, despite the odds weighing against success, I wished I was going with him – and from that brief reunion my resolve to take on the same voyage became set in stone and I said to myself 'I'm going to do this'.

My good friend Børge Ousland whose voyage in Northern Passage *determined me to attempt the same journey. Even before we'd met, Børge had invited me to join him on his trip, an offer I wished I could have taken up.*

*   *   *

Right from the start, however, there were any number of challenges that had to be overcome: finding sponsors, finding a crew who were sufficiently competent sailors but who were also able to contribute financially to the voyage, and last but by no means least, finding a boat.

Of the first of these issues, looking for sponsors proved to be more difficult than usual. A number of countries had supported the imposition of sanctions against Russia in punishment for its annexation of the Crimea, Britain among them. International companies are acutely sensitive to political uncertainties and are naturally reluctant to support projects where there is any likelihood of compromise. In our case, the chances of failure were high enough in themselves without suddenly finding ourselves caught up en route in some kind of international incident.

The indispensable Cheryl Lingard.

As I also learned from Børge, getting permits was difficult enough even in politically stable times, securing them now might be even more problematic.

Finding a crew might be less of a problem but without sponsors and without a boat, this was something that would have to wait. Besides, I was finding other commitments building up which made it necessary to look for someone who I could trust to project manage the whole trip.

In this I was extremely fortunate to find Cheryl Lingard, an employee of Somerset County Council from whom she secured an 18-month secondment. Cheryl proved a complete godsend, handling the nitty gritty details of the expedition, from dealing with insurance companies to tracking down what permits we would require, not only from the Russians but from the other countries through whose waters we were to sail.

This left me to look for a suitable boat.

*   *   *

As I've said earlier, while I've done my time on sailing boats, I don't count myself as a sailor in the same way as I am confident in my ability as a mountaineer and as a balloon pilot. The sea has a way of finding out those who take it on hoping for the best, and I've witnessed many other adventurers fail through over-confidence. I was also aware of just how costly the venture could be, and how easily it is to over-extend one's financial limits when it comes to purchasing and equipping boats. Small and compact as *Northern Passage* was, I'd heard Børge's trip had cost over 2.5 million Krone (about £250 000) which meant that, with a vessel sufficient for a crew of half a dozen or more, our expedition costs could be somewhere north of £1million.

While I envied Børge Ousland's fantastic endeavour in attempting the North West and North East Passages, I was also aware that such spartan conditions as portrayed in this photo aboard Northern Passage *would not be feasible for my attempt. With all the responsibilities and tensions that came with a larger and mixed crew, I knew I would need to find a vessel that offered slightly more breathing space. But a bigger boat also meant higher costs.*

Through the grapevine I'd heard of a boat lying up in Dublin, an Irish-built clipper that had sailed in the Antarctic, but on looking her over it was clear she'd seen better days. I reckoned she'd cost around half a million pounds to get in condition, and with sponsorship already proving difficult enough, for the boat alone coming up with such a large sum looked unfeasible.

The other thing against her was that no clipper type had been taken through the North East and North West Passages so I wasn't at all sure that this was the right type of boat for the Polar Ocean Challenge. Of course I'd sought advice from those sailors whom I knew and respected on the best kind of boat for our venture. Trouble is, you ask ten different people and you get ten different opinions – answers which suggested spending three times what you had in mind and in one case ten times that figure!

Abandoning the Dublin boat as being too tired to consider, I then took a trip up to Newcastle where I heard there was an 'ideal' prospect available for sale. Indeed the boat could not have had a better pedigree for it had previously been in the capable hands of yachtswoman, Dee Caffari, famed among many other exploits for her 2005 sailing solo the 'wrong way' around the world, against the prevailing winds and currents.

The vessel in which Dee Caffari became the first woman to sail solo around the world, now renamed Polar Bear, *was among the vessels I considered.*

Now renamed *Polar Bear*, this 72 foot 'Challenge 72' type steel-hulled vessel had survived three circumnavigations and, in 2009, had successfully competed in the Rolex Fastnet Race in support of the charity Earthwatch. *Polar Bear* had more recently been converted for arctic sailing, taking tourists to the Faeroes, Iceland and Greenland, but despite its illustrious past I did not consider her robust enough to survive the kind of ice we were likely to encounter.

It was at this point that a good friend of mine, Graham Hoyland, mentioned that he knew of a boat that, while not officially on the market, would be perfect for my enterprise and that the owner might be willing to sell. The boat was called *Northabout* and it was sitting in a boatyard in Westport, County Mayo, in the hands of its owner and builder, Jarlath Cunnane,

It sounded interesting and I asked Graham to travel to Westport, taking with him a boat surveyor in order to check the vessel out. I remember the phone call from Graham in which he first reported their findings. "Well Dave it's out of the water, and full of whiskey bottles!"

The surveyor's report suggested the boat needed a fair bit of work although when I called Jarlath to discuss the possible purchase his response was "Bejaysus! Turn the key and she's ready to go."

The indomitable Jaralath Cunnane.

Despite this typically fatalistic Irish response, and because of the surveyor's misgivings, I was hesitant about making an offer on the boat and asked Graham what his thoughts were. Now, Graham is a brilliant climber and sailor, he's made

It was Graham Hoyland, adventurer, mountaineer, sailor, film maker and author who suggested I take a look at Northabout *as a potential vessel for our voyage. We veteran explorers are a tight-knit group and if any of us needs advice or support, news soon gets out, and help is never far behind.*

Jarlath Cunnane's fascinating book tells the story of his voyage around the North Pole with seven fellow Irishmen.

wonderful films for the BBC, and his book, *Last Hours on Everest*, about Irving and Mallory's 1924 doomed ascent, is a classic, but he's not what I call a businessman.

In my own business career I've learnt the first price is never the best price and that negotiation is a natural part of buying and selling. You make an offer for half of what is being asked and haggle your way to a mutually acceptable compromise.

So when Graham said to me, "Look, Dave, just pay Jarlath the asking price – the goodwill will be worth it."

You must be joking! I thought to myself. "But Graham, if I do that, Jarlath will think we're complete idiots."

But Graham insisted. "I've met the guy. He built the boat. *Northabout* is his baby. Trust me, you'll get the best deal by going for the goodwill."

And so, against my better judgement, I said OK. And for the first time in my life I paid full price. *Northabout* was mine.

*   *   *

It's part of maritime lore that to change the name of a vessel brings bad luck. Not that this seems to have affected Dee Caffari's hugely successful career for the boat that became *Polar Bear* had undergone a number of name changes, usually in order to satisfy various sponsors. But *Northabout* sounded like a good name for our boat and, besides, there were added advantages in keeping her registered as an Irish vessel. The obvious alternatives would to be register her either in the country of our departure or at our last intended landfall, the United States. With both these countries being at the forefront of sanctions against the Russians keeping a more 'neutral' flag flying from our jackstaff might be no bad thing.

Also, as it now came to light, *Northabout* was already known to the Russians as she'd sailed through their waters in 2004/5. Thus keeping her name might oil the wheels when it came to securing our permits. Bearing in mind the wise words of the late President Nixon – "Don't change dicks in the middle of a screw." – *Northabout* she remained.

*   *   *

As things turned out we could hardly have found a better boat in which to undertake the Polar Ocean Challenge. The full story of our new boat's epic two-year sailing through the North East and North West Passages is told in Jarlath's own gripping book *Northabout*.

Built from scratch by Jarlath, *Northabout* is based on a 'Nadja 15' design by Frenchman Gilbert Caroff, specifically for sailing in polar waters. Fifteen metres in length and with a beam of 4.4 metres, she is cutter rigged, with a mainsail and two headsails set before the mast, carrying 185 square metres of sail – a 90HP Perkins diesel providing auxiliary power.

Importantly for sailing in shallow arctic waters *Northabout* was fitted with a retractable keelboard (for which we later added a hydraulic lift), with the engine being keel-cooled thus preventing debris being drawn into the engine block and causing major problems.

The design called for the hull to be either in steel or aluminium, with Jarlath choosing the latter due to its ease of handling during construction, its overall lighter weight, and advantage of not rusting.

This was the vessel in which Jarlath and his fellow seven crewmembers set out from Westport in June 2001 to sail the North West Passage. Surviving many adventures amid the shifting sea ice, *Northabout* reach Nome, Alaska in September of that year.

Three years later, in July 2004, the voyagers again weighed anchor to attempt the greater challenge of the North East Passage, a journey of twice the distance and against the prevailing currents. Again the *Northabout* and her crew proved equal to the task despite finding themselves several times trapped by ice. Eventually, finding their passage blocked by solid pack ice, *Northabout* overwintering while the crew returned to Ireland. In the summer of 2005 they rejoined their boat in order to resume their historic trip, *Northabout* arriving back in her home port in October, being the first small sailing vessel to successfully circumnavigate the polar ice cap from east to west.

The Northabout *sailing through ice during Jarlath's polar circumnavigation. As far as I was concerned the vessel had already earned her spurs regarding her basic construction, although it was quite clear that she would need to undergo a complete refit before I'd feel happy that she was ready to undertake the trip second time around.*

Jarlath's decision to build in aluminium rather than steel provided both strength and lightness to her hull and has surely given Northabout *many added years of useful life in the absence of rust.*

My investiture as High Sheriff of Wiltshire in Salisbury Cathedral, accompanied by my daughters, Alicia, Camilla and Amelia.

This was the boat that Graham had found laid up in Westport, now showing signs of a decade or more wear and tear and in need to some tender (and expensive) loving care. But Graham was a hundred percent right, the goodwill that came through my non-quibble purchase of the boat meant that my relationship with Jarlath could not have been better – a relationship that lasted well beyond our sailing *Northabout* on her first trip following her renovation, even surviving my calls from Russia in the middle of the night when things were going wrong.

Not that there was no comeback on agreeing to pay the asking price. I'm damn sure some of the costs during *Northabout*'s restoration were a little higher than normal as news got round Ireland about the Englishman who didn't know how to haggle!

*   *   *

Our original aim had been to set off in the midsummer of 2015. We got the boat back to Bristol early that year where our project manager, Cheryl Lingard, had been joined by Nick Martin, former Managing Director of RHM Foods. Nick was the perfect individual to bring on board – a perfectionist who insisted on all the boxes being ticked before he'd consider allowing a project to go 'live'. It was becoming clear by this date that we were running out of time but even so it came as a total surprise to me when Nick sent me an email saying that he was uncomfortable with giving the project the green light on the current timetable. His actual words were that we had 'a duty of care to the crew' and that in terms of safety we were not ready to go.

This came as a hammer blow to me, not only through the natural disappointment one feels at failure, but in knowing that a delay brought with it huge consequences, everything from the disruption caused to the crew's personal plans, the expectation of sponsors, through to inevitably increasing costs. Personally it meant that I could no longer take part in all four legs of the voyage as my impending appointment as High Sheriff of Wiltshire in March 2016 would require me to be at home for much of the year.

With a heavy heart I began the unenviable task of phoning all those involved in order to break the news. Underneath their acceptance of the situation I could hear the disappointment in each voice and I felt I'd let them down.

But it's funny how things work out. Within a few days a decision had been made that rather embarking on the intended voyage we would use the summer to undertake a 'shake down' cruise to Spitsbergen – a kind of sea trial for the boat, equipment, stores and her crew – in which we'd be able to prove our seaworthiness for the longer passage ahead.

Shake Down – On to Spitsbergen

We sailed *Northabout* from her Westport home up the Bristol Channel in September 2014. Here she was laid up in the boatyard at Sharpness for repairs and refitting with a view to beginning our Arctic voyage the following summer.

The scope of our intention for the expedition was by now taking firm shape, with the name Polar Ocean Challenge decided upon in order to attract interest from sponsors and potential crew. Now I needed to give some thought to establishing the bottom-line costs for the expedition, both in order to be able to talk figures with potential sponsors and to advise those who wished to join me on *Northabout* what kind of contribution they would be expected to make. While I was fully prepared to underwrite any shortfall personally, the need for professionalism in assessing the overall costs ran hand in hand with making sure the expedition functioned efficiently on a day-to-day basis as well as ensuring, as far as possible, our eventual success. Such planning of course applies to any venture, but more so for me on this expedition for, as Nick Martin had reminded me, here I was responsible for others, not just myself.

I have to admit, in some ways this need for meticulous planning ran counter to my previous practice and, to some extent, to my instincts. For even on non-solo expeditions, where one was climbing or treking with other professionals, each is reliant upon the other, for sure, but ultimately confident in one anothers' abilities. Sometimes, planning meant remembering to take a toothbrush.

I'm often asked about my views on the future of exploration now that every corner of our planet seems to accessible – an era in which mobile phones and GPS systems mean that one's every step can be followed and, potentially, rescue called in at a moment's notice. In contrast, one thinks of John Franklin and his men, marooned in a world of ice for years and literally lost to the world. Only conflict and political insecurity today prevent almost anyone going anywhere. And the risks of adventure, though by no means eliminated, are at least heavily mitigated.

On the other hand, not to make use of such technology would be foolhardy and thus 'Adventure Tourism', as it's become known, is an inevitable result. And while some may bemoan the loss of individualism in exploration, the upside is that more and more people can get to see the effect that mankind is having on the planet and maybe will begin to be more active in protecting and conserving our vulnerable landscapes and its flora and fauna. This was very much the motivation behind the Polar Ocean Challenge and in linking it with my charity

Sir Ernest Shackleton (1874-1922) is hailed as among the last of the true explorers in the period known as the Heroic Age of Antarctic Exploration. In the days before any communication with the outside world was possible, the story of his 1901 Trans Antarctic expedition aboard Endurance *remains one of the greatest epics of bravery and survival against the elements.*

With no chance of calling for help, and while the outside world awaited news of their fate, Shackleton and his men had to abandon Endurance, *her hull crushed by the ice. Spending weeks on the drifting ice sheet the party eventually took to the ship's boats to reach the comparative safety of Elephant Island. Twenty-two men waited while Shackleton and five others took one of the lifeboats (the now famous* James Caird) *and sailed to seek rescue. Shackleton arrived at the whaling station on South Georgia Island two weeks later, but because the whaling ships were not equipped to penetrate Antarctic sea ice it took Shackleton three months before he successfully approached Elephant Island in August 1916 and retrieved the rest of his crew on his third attempted rescue mission.*

I set up the charity Wicked Weather Watch in 2009 in order to provide a single source of information about global warming aimed specifically at children. The Polar Ocean Challenge offered the perfect opportunity to link the two projects and to highlight, through our voyage, the current state of ice melt in the polar region.

Wicked Weather Watch. This is not to say the Polar Ocean Challenge was any less extreme than other expeditions of which I'd been part and in some ways it could be said to contain even greater risks than, say, climbing Everest, for that had been achieved many times and the risks were known, while a polar circumnavigation in a single season would be a 'first'.

*   *   *

What the introduction of technology has also done is to make exploration much more expensive. In the past, even during my own time as an adventurer, it was possible to set off as an individual or small group in order to climb one of the world's highest peaks, to trek across the polar ice, or to explore the more remote parts of our planet, armed with the minimum essential equipment and with readily obtainable permits, if indeed they were necessary. Little thought was given to 'What Happened If' – and while such expeditions might end in failure, and sometimes tragically, for those taking part they truly represented the spirit of adventure.

Now, as the weeks ticked by, no one was more aware of the rising costs of our adventure, than I. The decision to delay for a year was likely to double my projected costs – costs that in no way could be passed on to those who had already signed up for various legs of the polar circumnavigation. These people had agreed to contribute their share of expenses for each leg of the voyage, sums that varied depending on how long they were aboard – bearing in mind that the costs of each leg differed as no two were of the same duration.

For instance the first leg, Bristol to Murmansk, represented about 20 per cent of the total cost, the second and longest leg, the North East Passage, around 35 percent, the third, the North West Passage, around 30 per cent, with the remainder being the cost of bring the boat back home. The skipper and first mate for the polar seas, at this stage yet to be signed up, would be the only paid crew.

On top of my original estimates I now had the costs of the Spitsbergen shake down cruise to add to my calculations.

Later on, after the Spitsbergen trip, such concerns as I may have had regarding the boat were alleviated by the firm and experienced hand of Steve Edwards. Steve had already expressed an interest in joining the Polar Ocean Challenge along with his wife and family and quite naturally wanted to ensure that *Northabout* would provide the safest possible vessel for that undertaking. An experienced sailor, Steve suggested we employ Colin Walker of Walker Planning & Construction to oversee the refitting of *Northabout* in preparation for the main voyage following our return from Spitsbergen.

Colin Walker.

Steve's intervention was a godsend to me as it relieved me of any concerns over the *Northabout*'s immediate seaworthiness and allowed time for me to track down the best possible skipper for sailing in polar waters. Equally of value was the fact the Steve brought on board (literally) his wife, Ros, a scientist whose interest in food and nutrition instigated a truly ground-breaking approach on how best to plan and put in place the foodstocks for our polar voyage – more of which later.

* * *

As the initial refitting continued at Sharpness, my efforts continued with the quest to find sponsors and also to recruit the crew who would take *Northabout* up to Spitsbergen and back.

So far my misgivings regarding sponsorship had proved well founded – times were hard in the corporate world and fewer of the multinationals were in the market for sponsorship deals. Overall, the days of money being freely handed over just because someone likes the idea of supporting a solo walk to the pole, or whatever, are long gone. These days sponsorship is part and parcel of big business and whole departments are given over to assessing the reciprocal benefits accrued through the support of a given project.

Fortunately I was able to rely on one or two close personal contacts for help, along with a number of smaller companies who supported Polar Ocean Challenge, chipping in with everything from fuel, solar panels and a water maker, to food

Magnus Day

Nikolai Litau

David H-A

Ben Edwards

Ros Edwards

Constance Difede

Barbara Fitzpatrick

Elouise Daniel

Steve Edwards

Crew members on the Svalbard Shake Down voyage.

and drink. Especially handy was a free supply of Mamont vodka when we welcomed our Russian skipper and first mate aboard later in the voyage. A personal essential on all my adventures is a supply of Ray Gray pork scratchings – salt to prevent cramp and packed with calories. A packet of pork scratchings and a Swiss Army Knife and you're set for life!

Finding the crew for the shake down cruise was less of a problem for while they need not necessarily comprise the same crew who would eventually take part in the Polar Ocean Challenge, it would definitely be an advantage to 'work up' the crew along with the boat. I would also need someone, an experienced sailor, who was able to recognise any of the vessel's defects or shortcomings in order to relay these to workers back at the boatyard.

Again I was able to rely on that small coterie of fellow explorers who passed the word around that I was looking for a crew and by late September 2015 *Northabout* was ready to sail north to Svalbard, the Norwegian archipelago that sits about halfway between continental Norway and the North Pole and of which Spitsbergen is the largest of the island group. This, to me, was the perfect opportunity to test the *Northabout*'s mettle in arctic waters and to discover what needed to be done to prepare her for the sterner test in the following year.

On 30 July the crew and I were part of a touching ceremony at which Major General Padre David Coulter blessed *Northabout*. Bristol's Mayor, George Ferguson, then honoured me by announcing my appointment as an ambassador for the city's European Green Challenge initiative, saying "I am sure that David will be able to use this daring journey to further raise the profile and encourage us all to work that much harder to combat climate change. I wish him and his team the best of luck on this challenging voyage and the educational benefits that it will bring to the city's children." Indeed, the Mayor had been extremely generous in providing harbourside facilities which regrettably were withdrawn when Mr Ferguson's tenure as Mayor ended.

Saturday 1 August found me last-minute shopping at the marine stores and that night ten of us slept on board *Northabout* ready for a 7.00am start. Slipping off for

Northabout *with the familiar skyline of Bristol beyond; a city which had been so kind, generous and supportive of the Polar Ocean Challenge.*

an early morning ablute in the nearby toilets rather than using the ship's offices avoiding treating Bristol dock as a main sewer.

At last we cast off from the floating dock, passing through the swing bridge and the lock gates and heading downriver towards the Bristol Channel, making for Oban. There's few feelings quite like setting off on a voyage, anxiety balanced by anticipation, and on a beautiful day such as this all aboard were in good heart. In

All aboard! The crew pose with the Mayor of Bristol, George Ferguson, who proved a loyal friend to Northabout *and the aims of the Polar Ocean Challenge which dovetailed nicely with the city's European Green Challenge initiative.*
From left: Ros Edwards, Mimi Edwards, Steve Edwards, myself, Barbara Fitzpatrick, George Ferguson, Constance Difede, Nikolai Litau, Magnus Day and Ben Edwards.

On the morning of Sunday 2 August 2015 the Northabout *slips quietly out of the docks on the start of her voyage to Svalbard.*

the distance, landward, rose the dark outline of the Brecons and Black Mountains – so familiar to me from my schooldays and now almost more majestic when viewed from the sea.

Sadly, the tranquility was short lived for the next morning, off the Irish coast, I came up on watch to find *Northabout* bouncing all over the place, with Nikolai having pulled the reef, deciding to use the motor to get through the shipping lanes – and with Barbara, Steve, Ben and Constance all being horribly ill – leaving only Nikolai, Magnus and myself to manage the boat.

Beside getting to know *Northabout*, the shake down cruise was also a good opportunity for the crew to get to know one another. While not all those on board

A golden start to the voyage.

Magnus teaching Ben the ropes during the shake down. The voyage gave the crew a chance to get to know each other as well as familiarising themselves with Northabout. Though by no means a complete novice, ocean sailing was new to Ben who, at fourteen, was the youngest on board as well as the only crew who intended to complete all four legs. Earlier that year Ben and his mother, Ros, had helmed aboard a 35-foot yacht from Port Solent to the Isle of Wight as preparation for taking the RYA Competent Crew Course. Throughout the Polar Ocean Challenge I watched Ben's progress with great interest and admired him greatly, starting off a boy and returning as a man.

would be taking on the Polar Ocean Challenge, several crew members had signed up for one or more of the four legs, with young Ben Edwards aiming to complete the whole trip.

For the Svalbard voyage I had appointed Magnus Day as skipper. In his late thirties, Magnus had been sailing professionally for a dozen years, including trips in antarctic waters. His first mate on *Northabout* was the Russian sailor, Nikolai Litau – eventually to prove a key figure in the success of Polar Ocean Challenge.

Nikolai (Nikolay) was born in 1955 in North Kazakstan. After serving in the Soviet Army he attended university in Moscow and, aged 32, began life as a sailor eventually getting his skipper's ticket. From 1996 to 1999 as captain of the yacht *Apostol Andrey* Nikolai successfully navigated the Northern Sea Route, becoming the first to sail round the world in the meridian direction. For this he was awarded the Medal for Seamanship, formerly given to, among others, Sir Francis Chichester, Sir Robin Knox Johnston, Alain Bombard and other famous yachtsmen. In 2002 he became the first to navigate of the Northeast Passage on a yacht and subsequently took the *Apostol Andrey* on further circumnavigations of the globe. In all Nikolai has surpassed 150 000 miles under sail and, later, sailing under his command, I could only admire his ability to detect even slight changes in the

Nikolai Litau aboard the Northabout. *Note the Irish flag, maintained as part of the vessel's registration – a prudent move to avoid any difficulties resulting from tensions between Britain and Russia at the time.*

We have now left Rosslare where we stayed when cowering from the scary wind. We've just reached the Mull of Kintyre in Scotland and hope to reach Ardfern by early tomorrow morning. The best thing of all about yesterday though was that I started using sea-sickness tablets and am still feeling fine. I also, after an unforgivably long time, realised why making tea on the onboard cooker is so tricky. It's not on gimbals, which usually keep the cooker the right way up if the boat is heeled over. For those of you who have a gruesome fascination with how diffi-cult it is to go to the toilet in bad weather sailing gear on a floor that's at a 45 degree angle at two in the morning I must disappoint you. It's not that tricky. Making the tea is harder.

wind that might signal a change in sea state, and his uncanny ability always to appear to sleep with one eye open – instantly alert to a alterations in *Northabout*'s movements or her engine missing a beat.

While, on the shake down cruise, Nikolai was acting as second in command to Magnus, but the benefits of having a Russian speaker on board for the more test-ing voyage ahead was becoming clear to me. Nikolai's proven successes in sailing arctic waters would undoubtedly relieve some of the anxieties regarding our safe passage and, not only that, how much easier it would make my life to have a native Russian on hand when it came to seeking permits!

On the down side would someone with his experience become a problem when it came to making overall decisions regarding the Polar Ocean Challenge? In his native country Nikolai was famous, a hero, and would he be reluctant to put his reputation at risk for a bunch of British adventurers? And, while I had every confidence in myself as a decision maker, in the last resort would Nikolai be amendable to taking orders from me?

Taking the bull by the horns, and aware of the fact that on his own navigations of both the North East and North West passages Nikolai had been obliged to over-winter, I ask him point blank on his thoughts on our chances of making it through in a single season.

"No way," was his immediate response. But after a vodka or two, he agreed that it might be possible, and that he would – for a fee – sign on as skipper for the Polar Ocean Challenge, with his colleague Denis Davydov as first mate.

*   *   *

On our second day out the Irish Sea reminded us all of who was in charge. With the Shipping Forecast warning of a Force 9 gale, Magnus and I decided to head for Rosslare as a safe haven until the storm passed. There we tied up among the fishing boats until the following day when the weather improved, although a brisk wind remained. We poled out the genoa, giving *Northabout* her head, and sailed like a dream all day. In 24 hours we covered 160 nautical miles although we were surprised by the amount of traffic in the shipping lanes and only narrowly avoided one cargo ship thanks to Nikolai's quick action at the helm.

Friday 7 August found us in the lovely little Scottish harbour at Ardfern where we wolfed down a full English breakfast and enjoyed the pleasures of free toilets and showers on shore. Here we were able to fix the genoa pole that had been giving problems and also took on board a massive sea anchor that I'd arranged to pick up and which, along with so many other adaptations to *Northabout,* proved to be a godsend on our later voyage.

It's getting noticeably lighter as we sail north, passing Sumburgh Head at the tip of the Orkneys, and though blessed with fine weather *Northabout* continued to throw at us numerous little niggles that required fixing, or notes to be made for improvements on our return to Sharpness. Nikolai again proved his value by fixing minor mechanical issues – a skill learnt while working as a mechanic in Russia. On 9 August we were able to repay him by helping to celebrate his 60th birthday as we landed in Lerwick – fish and chips and lobster!

Somehow or other I'd injured my knee earlier in the trip and this was now playing up, helped by taking painkillers but reminding me of how small injuries could have a big impact on this sort of adventure. However my mind was taken off this by the pleasure of catching up with an old schoolfriend, Maureen, who brought some reporters and a gaggle of schoolchildren down to look around *Northabout*. They also brought heaps of wonderful food that kept us going for a several days after we'd left Lerwick – such wonderful hospitality. Lerwick also gave us the first opportunity to test our camera drone, flying it over the harbour and town.

Next stop Tromso which we hoped to reach after five or six days at sea. But not long out of Lerwick the engine starts to misfire and eventually comes to a stop. While we continue under sail, Magnus and Nikolai disappear into the confined depths of the engine compartment and within the hour have it running happily

Nikolai relied on his computer for much of his navigational work and his records covering his previous voyages in the polar regions were of vital importance to our impending expedition.

Our last fish and chip supper before leaving Lerwick on the evening of 10 August. From left: Constance, Barbara, Ben, Magnus and myself.

again. A blocked filter due to contaminated fuel – another reminder of how small things can result in major difficulties. Lucky we fixed the genoa pole when we did!

We begin to sight oil rigs, at night standing out like distant mirrored cities ablaze with light. Even some miles off one can smell the sharp tang of oil and gas on the wind.

Bumpy headwinds as we approach the Norway coast and as we near Tromso we motor up through the channel past stunning scenery, idyllic coastal villages perched at the edge of the shoreline. The following day is equally gorgeous and everyone goes ashore, odds jobs to be done along with replenishing of stocks, and a visit to the Polar Museum. Somehow I manage to leave my phone on the dock-side where someone has run off with it – very annoying – reported it at the police station but little chance of recovery.

I caught a bus to the airport to meet Ellie Daniel who had flown in to take over as cook aboard *Northabout*. We originally intended to top up the fuel tanks here but discovered that oil is twice the price we paid in Scotland and decided to wait and fill up again in Lerwick.

SHIP'S LOG
13 August 2015 – DHA aboard Northabout

Grand day, dry. Up at 3.30. Very tired. Watch was nice. Always quieter than the afternoon watch. Off land. Saw the odd oil well derrick. Poled genoa out so good progress, 6-7 knots through the water.
Beef Bourginon for dinner. Very nearly tempted by wine. Into the rhythm. Learnt how to whip a piece of rope. Bed early. Then P bottle slipped!

Ben and Magnus celebrate crossing the Arctic Circle while Nikolai insists the crew toasts the occasion with a traditional drink – two shots of vodka and one of seawater!

August 19 finds us at sea again, the last leg to Spitsbergen. Poor Ellie is very seasick and confined to her bunk. An extra body on board means that Magnus and I share the same bunk on and off watch and the crew decide a washing up rota is required, which is put in place. The following day we are past Bear Island which lies roughly halfway between Norway and Svalbard and by the morning of 22 August we could see the glaciers on the coast as we sailed serenely into the bay at Svalbard's largest settlement, Longyearbyen, on Spitsbergen.

But here disaster struck. As *Northabout* edged towards her mooring, Steve jumped from the deck on to the plastic pontoon, bow line in hand, and fell. It was immediately obvious that this was serious. Steve's face was white with pain and it was pretty obvious he'd broken his leg. While the anxious crew members, including Ben, helped make Steve as comfortable as possible I went off in search of the island's medical centre – only to be greeted by an administrator who announced that the hospital was closed until 4.00pm! As it was by now only noon you can imagine my reaction and, indeed, once Steve was produced from the insides of a local taxi, even she realised the need for rapid action. An X-ray confirmed two fractures in Steve's tibia which required plating and thus a flight back to the UK the following day.

Maybe the accident unnerved Nikolai for he confided in me some misgivings about our future attempt on the North East Passage. While he was keen, he felt the crew lacked experience – yet as he spoke it became clear he simply wanted me to appreciate the extreme difficulties of what lay ahead, recognising that as expedition leader I should be made fully aware of my responsibilities. His concern was a gesture of friendship and, looking back, this moment was perhaps one of the most important things to come out of our shake down voyage.

Ben and Ellie as Northabout *sails from Tromso on to Svalbard.*

SHIP'S LOG
23 August 2015 – DHA aboard
Northabout

Up at 5.30 to get to Steve for 6.00am. Take him to the airport. Poor guy, lots of pain...
Walked back with Nikolai. He's worried we are not experienced enough for the N.E. Passage, but keen to do it.

Glaciers off the Svalbard coast.

BEN EDWARDS' BLOG
25 August 2015

Upon leaving Longyearbyen we noticed that there were a lot of seals in the fjord. I looked in the book on wildlife in Svalbard and I think that they were Harbour Seals. Actually, Svalbard's wildlife was a big part of the day yesterday. When we are anchored, if you go outside, you have to have a good look around to see if there are any polar bears It's slightly unnerving, having to, when you leave your house, make sure that you aren't about to be attacked by a bear. Although we do have methods for repelling bear attacks, we have guns, obviously. Although before this trip started I was asked by a surprisingly large number of people, but you wouldn't actually shoot a polar bear would you? Unfortunately the answer to that question is: if it was running towards me then yes, I would shoot a bear. However, we don't just have guns, we have a hand held fog horn to scare it off and we have a wonderful thing called Bear Spray, brilliant! It's just really really strong pepper spray that you are supposed to use on Polar Bears. It's not very nice for the bear but it's better than shooting it.

As far as I was concerned the cruise to Svalbard had more than proved its worth. Apart from Steve's accident the passage had been without major incident and *Northabout* had revealed both her capabilities and shortcomings. I'd also been able to observe the characters of my fellow crew members and to come to decisions regarding their capabilities and shortcomings too. Most importantly, I'd formed a close friendship and deep mutual respect for Nikolai who, while expressing his concerns, also recognised that my imperatives might necessitate a contrary course of action to his. Nikolai would be our skipper for the voyage to come.

The next two weeks were spent exploring the islands in the Svalbard group, glacier gazing, sailing through ice and getting to know the local wildlife, using the RIB to take parties on shore to explore secluded inlets and sandy coves.

The tiny settlement of Ny-Ålesund on the island of Spitsbergen.

Northabout *among the ice.*

Nikolai left us as had been arranged, and various others joined the crew, those who had paid to spent a little holiday time on *Northabout* along with future crew members who had signed up for one or more of the four legs. These included Ros Edwards and her daughter Mimi.

*   *   *

In retrospect, the shake down, which had first appeared to me as a huge disappointment and a headache in meeting ever-rising costs, turned out to be the platform from which the success of the Polar Ocean Challenge later sprang. I can say with some confidence that the later voyage if not ending in failure, would certainly have been beset with problems that would have made the passage in a single season quite unlikely. From the tiniest niggles in the galley, to the major issues with the engine, we now had a chance to iron these out.

A polar bear's breakfast. Magnus, Nikolai and myself examine the bloody remains of a walrus.

With the return of the vessel to Sharpness, and armed with a lengthy 'To Do' list, Colin Walker had six months or so to prepare *Northabout* for her voyage of circumnavigation.

And so *Northabout* was sailed in to the dry dock at Sharpness where work could begin. The starting point was to make sure the fuel system was clean and reliable

Northabout *in dry dock at Sharpness and the fitting of the new propeller which increased its efficiency by around 10 per cent.*

so we removed all the old fuel, cleaned the tanks and installed a dual filter system, that means if one filter got clogged we could easily switch over to the 2nd filter.

The shake down voyage had provided an opportunity to make some precise calculations over fuel use. While I intended to sail as much as possible I needed to make sure there was enough fuel for the Eastern Passage and having checked the existing fuel capacity we found we had 5 tanks which gave 1850ltrs of fuel, so we then added another 300ltr of emergency fuel in the stern locker. In order to manage the fuel and control the flow from each tank, we installed a manifold and a day tank, which would allow us to easily isolate a tank should it get contaminated when re-fuelling. The engine was given a full service and all the pipework replaced.

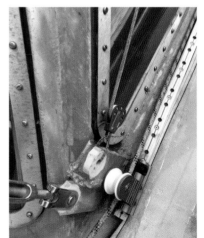

Northabout was fitted with a lifting keel but the old system had proved to be very unreliable and so Sharpness Boatyard came up with a clever hydraulic lifting system that would hold the keel in place.

All the crew would be taking laptops, tablets and phones and at one point on the shake down, with everyone's devices charging or connected, we had managed to fry the electronics. So we re-wired the boat and checked the inverter so we could be sure to have a reliable 24 volt supply for the bread maker and microwave oven which Ros had intelligently suggested we take. We needed to make sure there was sufficient power for the general day-to-day use of the boat, plus all the electronics, so we doubled the storage capacity of the domestic batteries and installed a small independent generator. This meant we could generate power from the alternator on the main engine, or by using the new generator, or by the solar panels installed on the deck.

All the electronics on the boat were upgraded to give reliable boat speed, wind direction and depth, and a new Raymarine solid state radar unit was installed in order to spot icebergs. Two satellite communication systems were also fitted to allow us to keep in touch with the outside world and, more importantly, to gather the latest weather and ice information.

The anchor winch had to be replaced and upgraded as the original had burned out when attempting to lift the new anchor we'd picked up in Ardfern. A new propeller and shaft was also fitted, the rudder repaired, the hull anti-fouled and all the rigging checked and upgraded.

We purchased and installed a new water maker from the manufactueres who'd kindly loaned one for the Svalbard trip. This, for me, was the device that saved our later expedition for without it I don't believe we would have made it successfully. Water tanks take up an enormous amount of space and, when filled, add huge weight to the boat. Already fully loaded with fuel there was simply not

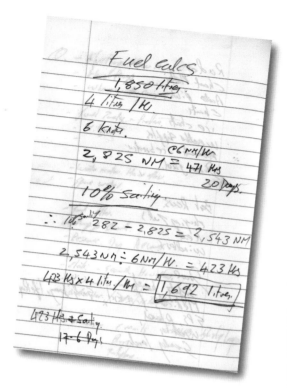

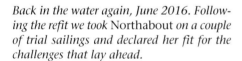

A page from Northabout's *log book with my calculations for fuel use.*

Back in the water again, June 2016. Following the refit we took Northabout *on a couple of trial sailings and declared her fit for the challenges that lay ahead.*

enough room to carry all the water needed for drinking, cooking, cleaning and so on. That water maker saved our bacon.

For additional comfort a lot of carpentry work was carried out, new insulation added while the storage area around the boat was maximised so we could store three months' worth of food, including emergency provisions.

Finally, with crew safety in mind we installed a liferaft bracket on the transom to secured a 10-man liferaft and purchased two 15hp 2-stroke outboards for the inflatable which could be used to help pull the boat off the ice if needed.

By late spring 2016 *Northabout* was a completely renewed vessel – literally ship-shape and Bristol fashion – and ready to take on the Polar Ocean Challenge.

First Leg – To Murmansk

Shipshape and Bristol fashion. Northabout on the morning of departure. The newly fitted liferaft bracket on the transom can clearly be seen along with the two outboards for the inflatable – results of Steve Edwards' improvements to on-board safety.

And so, with *Northabout* now fully fettled – with Nikolai confirmed as skipper and his compatriot, Denis Davydov as first mate (joining the boat in Murmansk along with our Russian permits) – having told the world what we were up to, it was indeed time for the off. The only thing that was missing, was me!

In 2016 I had the honour of being appointed High Sheriff of Wiltshire, a position that one holds for a year. Had things gone to plan the Polar Ocean Challenge would have now been over, but the year's delay meant I was still fulfilling the many engagements the role of High Sheriff demands and therefore had to forego taking part in the first leg and last legs of the voyage. Likewise Nikolai was unavailable to join the boat until Lerwick on the first leg.

Luckily, Steve Beacham, owner of the dry dock at Sharpness was friendly with Thornbury Sailing Club and he got in touch with Annie Green, then Commodore of the club, in the first instance to help get the boat from Bristol up to Sharpness. Annie agreed to organise a few hands which was of enormous help for the Bristol Channel represented one of the trickiest sailing challenges of the whole voyage.

A packed boat leaving Bristol 16 June 2016. I recall it was a pretty grim day, grey, cold and raining. Those on board are l-r: Annie Green, John Harvey, Ben Edwards, Steve Edwards, Hazel Richards, Mimi Edwards, myself, Ros Edwards, Dave Cushing, Barbara Fitzpatrick, John Whiteley.

With the world's second highest tidal range and ever-shifting mudbanks it is not a passage to be trifled with.

And so, on 19th June 2016, I met with Annie and other sailing club members at the SS *Great Britain* any one of whom could have navigated the channel but in the end Dave Cushing took over as skipper, sailing *Northabout* first to Avonmouth and then on to Sharpness. I was delighted to have on board for this short trip a good friend, Lord John Cope, whose former parliamentary constituency was Northavon, the border of which we now sailed alongside, with *Northabout* trailing her wake far beneath the arched girders of Brunel's bridge suspended high above us over the Avon Gorge.

Just three short days before I had been facing the press, telling them about the Polar Ocean Challenge and Wicked Weather Watch and emphasising the serious purpose of our voyage, bringing the effects of rapid global warming in the arctic to the world's attention.

Earlier, and just as we'd done the year before, I asked my friend the Revd David Coulter to come down to Sharpness to bless the boat. I confess to being a little superstitious and as I stood on board *Northabout* while David performed the simple service of blessing both boat and crew, I somehow knew that we were going to make it.

The media at Sharpness.

*　　　*　　　*

Chaplain General David Coulter holds a service of blessing for boat and crew.

Because I was unable to take part in the first leg, and Nikolai also, Annie Green, her husband and other members of Thornbury Sailing Club agreed to take *Northabout* up to Lerwick – a fantastic help to me but, I'm sure, a pleasurable challenge for them also. And so the crew comprised Dave Cushing as skipper, the young Ben Edwards, Annie Green and her husband John, John Whiteley, Hazel Richards and David Marshall. Steve Edwards was to remain on board until Tromsö, primarily responsible for checking the newly installed electronics and associated communications gear.

Almost immediately, and despite all our care in refitting and in taking the vessel on trial to test her seaworthiness, the crew was met with potential disaster – a few hours into the voyage and *Northabout* was sinking!

Sailing through St George's Channel, just off the Welsh coast, water began to fill the bilges and it became clear that the pumps were not able to keep ahead of the inflow. Unable to determine the cause and make repairs at sea, Dave Cushing wisely made a bee line for Holyhead. After frantic emails and phone calls, I managed to get hold of the Sharpness boatyard who, in turn, were able to identify and

The first leg from Bristol to Murmansk involved stops at Holyhead for repairs, picking up Nikolai in Lerwick and dropping off Steve in Tromsö.

Northabout in Holyhead harbour waiting for repairs.

BEN EDWARDS' BLOG
21 June 2016

I went on watch at ten and not much happened. When I got off watch it was discovered that we had two or three inches of water in the bottom of the boat which shouldn't be there. Dad and Dave tried to fix this but, as it turned out, our bilge pumps are broken, yay! It was decided that we would head to Wales and get some guys from Sharpness up to fix it for us. So we headed east and we've docked in the Holyhead marina. We called Sharpness and then we went to bed (they arrived at 23:20 and worked until about 1.30).

Dolphins entertain the crew as Northabout *approaches the Scottish coast.*

JOHN WHITELEY'S BLOG*
22 June 2016

On the way round Wales a few snags occurred and an overnight in Holyhead was ordered. Began to remember a few nautical terms and as familiarity with the other unknown crew depended the flavour of this new adventure heightened. Good set of fellow swashbucklers and a damn good cook. The press-ganged skipper is cool – calm and the techy is a wizard. Good stuff.

Dolphins gambol merrily to port and starboard and all manner of seabirds swoop and yelp around our ship. As the sea swell increases with white horses riding the crest... the crew settle confidently into routines. Happy days!

As the Shetlands come into view a small wave of sadness washes over me in realisation that this short sojourn is closing.

*John crewed from Bristol to Lerwick.

fix the problem. It turned out the stern gland (essentially the bearing which allows the propeller shaft to exit through the bottom of the boat without letting the water enter) was leaking like a sieve and this, along with the pumps being incorrectly assembled, was the problem.

Nor were these the only difficulties the crew encountered on their way up to Lerwick, and each day I received a progress report that more often than not would flag up yet another problem. These ranged from minor niggles with the engine and electronics, to the cooker not working properly, and the water maker playing up. I thanked my lucky stars that the Thornbury people were on board for they were well used to dealing with the sort of things small boats were always likely to throw at you – which meant that Ben and the other less experienced sailors were in good hands.

In fact, one can see from the daily blogs that a number of crew members put up on the Polar Ocean Challenge website, several were quite relieved to be able to spend a few hours in Holyhead as some of them had suffered from seasickness and had yet to find their sea legs.

For me, however, back on dry land, there was added frustration. Every day we lost in getting to Murmansk weighed against making the whole trip in a single season. And while the crew on each leg could not be faulted for playing their part in our success, the fact that there were regular crew changes for each leg, did

I think, inevitably dilute the sense of urgency and focus that would have come from a unchanged crew undertaking the whole voyage. And on occasions I did need to remind myself that this adventure was different from my earlier expeditions on which achieving the goal was fundamental to the challenge. Here, for most of those taking part, it was the journey itself that was the thing.

It also came home to me how vital was the use of social media on this trip, especially with Ben on board whose generation is completely at home with this form of communication. Keeping the voyage in the public eye, Ben was able to provide our followers on the Polar Ocean Challenge website with daily reports on events aboard *Northabout* – likewise with Wicked Weather Watch and Ben's chosen charities which were benefitting from his trip. It's amazing how much one can read into these communications, sometimes unintended revelations about the state of the boat and crew – informative for me during those legs when I was languishing on dry land.

John Whiteley preparing his blog.

*   *   *

Northabout sailed into Lerwick on the morning of 27 June. By this time Steve had pretty much got to grips with the communications equipment but, worryingly, the stern gland continued to leak and I had to arrange for an engineer based in Lerwick to sort it out. The bearing was eventually re-engineered and gave no further trouble for the whole of the trip and thankfully, and satisfyingly, the shopping list of things to be fixed was by now getting smaller.

HAZEL RICHARDS' BLOG
22 June 2016

The Hebrides are stunning, the cove had a pub in it but it was too far to swim! I have only had one bout of sea sickness leaving the Bristol Channel and I thank Steve for taking over my 2am to 6am watch duties!

We have been travelling for over two weeks now and I declare I have well and truly found my sea legs! We experienced our worst weather with rolling waves and bitter cold winds. On calmer days, I loved nothing more than to sit on the back corners seats feeling the boat rise above the waves, roll, toss and turn.

Lerwick harbour.

Hazel Richards, who had signed on for the trip to Norway, taking in the sun on deck.

ROS EDWARDS' BLOG
29 June 2016
on a train in London

It is a week before I join Northabout *in Tromsö. I'm sitting on a train on the way into London. It's 7.35am. The boat is in Lerwick getting some much needed TLC.*

I have been collecting a ton of food, literally, to provision Northabout *for the North East and North West Passages. 16kg of hot chocolate, 20kg of Parmesan, and around 100 packets of biscuits – you have to get your priorities right! With a ton of food sitting in the hall visitors have been asking if we're expecting the apocalypse. I am so excited! Sitting in London imagining the water and ice and isolation – a reality dislocation. When I'm on the boat I won't give a second thought to my priorities for today – they just won't seem that important.*

Ben again played an excellent ambassadorial role by visiting the school in Lerwick while the crew stocked up on things ashore. Here Dave Marshall and John Whiteley, reluctantly, bade farewell to their fellow mariners to return home, while Nikolai arrived to take over as skipper. Again my shore-based responsibilities were put to the test when I got a phone call to say that Nikolai had left his computer containing all his navigational charts – vital for the future – in the airport terminal at Inverness! Frantic phone calls resulted in my Scots friend, Malcolm Offord, persuading a colleague in Inverness to collect the laptop and arrange for DHL to get it to Lerwick.

On 2 July, with stern flange and bilge pumps replaced, *Northabout* sailed north for her next port of call, Tromsö. Those already aboard were clearly settling in to the routines essential to the good management of a vessel at sea and, with Nikolai now in command, it seemed to us all that departing Scotland signalled the start of our adventure for real.

Once again the spectral flare from the oil rigs provided waymarks for the night watches aboard *Northabout*, but the undoubted highlight for the crew on this leg was the crossing of the Arctic Circle. I was delighted to see from the blogs that the traditional celebration was followed, the crew taking a slug of seawater and two of vodka to toast the gods of these northern waters. Champagne was also taken! Ben did a little piece to camera for ITN and Hazel found her phone got reception and so called her husband back in England.

By now the nights were getting shorter and the thin ribbon of land off to starboard signalled the approach of the Norwegian coast. Two days later, on 7 July, *Northabout* nosed her way through the coastal inlets towards the busy port of Tromsö.

Here the crew were able to spend some time off the boat enjoying the hospitality offered by the city and its friendly people and restocking some food and other essentials. Ros had flown in with her daughter Bea and the Edwards family made the most of the quiet luxury of a hotel, Ben catching up on sleep between feasting on, as his blog records, excellent local pizza. Here *Northabout* was to bade her farewells to Steve, with his wife Ros now joining the crew for the second leg – the North East Passage.

With Ros came the installation of a microwave with a built-in convection oven, part of her meticulous planning for ensuring the crew were properly fed during the most arduous legs of the voyage. John Harvey, husband of Annie Green, had 'volunteered' to be responsible for provisioning the boat on the first leg and also took on the role of principal cook, a job made more hazardous by the faulty gas oven that was condemned by an engineer in Lerwick, leaving just the gas rings available. Ros had also insisted on a breadmaking machine which overcame the problem of storing bread on board which quickly became mouldy.

HAZEL RICHARDS' BLOG
5 July 2016

We had champagne on ice to mark our crossing of the Arctic Circle and made sure we gave some to Neptune to keep Northabout *safe on her onward journey. It was a perfect day, the sun shone. We are now heading for Tromsö, meandering through the beautiful Fjords. So what am I looking forward to next... a shower in Tromsö and resupply of the tucker as we only have our Leader's pork scratchings left!*

Dr John Harvey, principal cook aboard Northabout *on the first leg. Denied the use of the faulty oven, everything had to be prepared on the two gas rings before Ros introduced the microwave in Tromsö. This photo graphically illustrates the compact conditions of the galley on board.*

Steve and Nikolai checking the navigation and comms gear in Tromso.

These two devices made significant calls on the vessel's electricity supply and on the electric generator that now also needed attention.

While I was making last-minute arrangements to fly to Murmansk, forever aware that time was not on our side, I was urging the crew to make a start for North Cape but Nikolai emailed to say that the parts needed to repair the generator had not turned up and, worse, just as *Northabout* had finished refuelling, the steering gear jammed and they had to return to dock. Once again Nikolai's

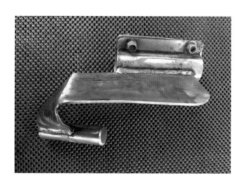

The cause of the jammed rudder.

Ros and Dave Cushing on the stormy passdage around North Cape.

brilliant engineering skills came to the rescue in what would otherwise have been a lengthy and costly repair. And as far as the generator was concerned, John agreed to wait for the parts to arrive and fly with them up to Vardo, a small port on the Norwegian coast roughly halfway to Murmansk, where he'd meet up again with the boat.

The fishing port of Vardo was an unscheduled port of call but a necessary one in order for the replacement generator parts to be delivered while still on the European mainland. It was where Hazel arranged to leave the boat before entering Russian waters and also gave the crew a brief respite ashore after a rough trip around North Cape. North-about can be seen rubbing shoulders alongside fishing boats at the pontoon.

55

The weather as they approached North Cape (Nordkapp) on 10 July rapidly deteriorated, high winds and freezing spray. Several aboard were seasick, making watch-keeping an arduous two-hour stint and their arrival in Vardo on the morning of 11 July gave the crew a welcome respite. John arrived with the generator parts which Nikolai replaced while others explored the little town, a major fishery centre and reeking of fish, before visiting the museum and catching up on communications with friends and family back home.

On 14 July *Northabout* sailed into Murmansk successfully concluding an eventful first leg of Polar Ocean Challenge.

Nikolai's evocative photo taken on 11 July in Vardo. Across the harbour lie some of the town's many derelict buildings – many adorned with graffiti. Sea Fever recalls Masefield's poem, a favourite with all yachtsmen who share his passion for 'the lonely sea and the sky.'

Second Leg – The North East Passage

My departure from England to fly up to Murmansk was not without the usual flurry of last-minute rearrangements and constant references to my hastily scribbled lists of 'Things to Do'. These included everything from the mundane 'pack paperbacks' to the more critical issues relating to finances and permits for the trip ahead – and of course making sure that all my domestic arrangements at home were in order during my absence.

And so, on 13 July, I flew into Murmansk and took a hotel room to await the arrival of *Northabout* the following day. The crew sailed her in to the commercial dock where she looked tiny surrounded by huge container ships and, after the immigration people had inspected her, the crew were able to come ashore.

Visitors are left in no doubt that Murmansk is a working city – a coal port dusted with a layer of grime and with no facilities for leisure craft. One by one the crew took the fifteen minute walk through the city streets so they could take advantage of a welcome shower at my hotel.

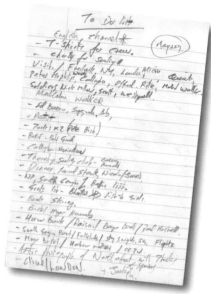

One of several pages of 'To Do' lists at the front of my Northabout *Log Book. There are reminders for everything from getting T-Shirts made up for the crew, to visiting the dentist.*

BEN EDWARDS' BLOG
14 July 2016

We came into Murmansk while I was asleep and woke up when the immigration people came on board. There's something very unsettling about having four people who you don't know, speaking a language you don't understand, getting you to sign lots of bits of paper that will allow you to stay in their country.

Murmansk – a view across the harbour.

But as we soon found out, while the city itself had a workaday look about it, the people could not have been more friendly and helpful – a characteristic I've found in so many of these remote northern communities, with their 'can-do' attitude and true communal spirit.

This enterprising character could not have been better exemplified as a result of the discussion that Nikolai and I had almost as soon as I'd got off the plane. My preoccupation throughout the planning of our voyage had been with ensuring that we had the best possible information regarding the state of sea ice and the weather ahead of us. If *Northabout* was to make it through both the North East and North West Passages in a single season, we would need to take advantage of every opportunity to sail through open water and breaking ice created by seasonal melt and by storms.

Murmansk's impressive memorial to the Defenders of the Soviet Arctic during World War Two and (inset) the eternal flame.

DAVID H-A'S BLOG
14 July 2016

Murmansk has historical connections to the Arctic ocean that goes back hundreds of years. We all probably know Murmansk from the Arctic convoys and the massive sacrifice of the Second World War. Russia lost more people than all of the other nations put together, so they rightly honour their dead. The people here have an in-depth hardiness in their DNA. They have that frontier town 'can do' attitude – and that includes their frigging mosquitoes!

We knew we could obtain information from the Russian Ice Service which, every two days, sent out reports on current conditions on the Northern Sea Route. My concern, however, was that predicting a clear passage ahead was so critical to our success that a daily update was essential. To this end I suggested that we subscribe to a service provided by an agency based in St Petersburg through which daily ice reports could be received – to which Nikolai, as only a Russian can, expressed a view that only a fool would agree to pay for such data!

Instead, he suggested, that we visit his good friend Sergei – a fisherman and a mean hand with a barbecue he told me – who, for a couple of bottles of scotch would be able to provide all and more that St Petersburg could offer. I hesitated at this point, partly because the only Sergei I'd come across before was the little meerkat character who advertised car insurance and, try as I might, every time Nikolai mentioned his friend's name, the meerkat's image popped into my head.

Ye of little faith! We travel out to Sergei's dacha where he's indeed prepared a superb fish barbecue with a wonderful spread, including of course beer and vodka. Among other guests was a former professor whose English was immaculate and now acted as a tour guide on Russia's famous nuclear powered icebreaker, the first of its kind. And now Nikolai played his trump card. Sergei, it turns out, worked for the Murmansk Shipping Company in charge of providing information for all their tankers and icebreakers operating on the Northern Sea Route for which he provided daily ice and weather reports.

Sergei Deyneka (right) and Vladimir Blinov with the remains of the barbecue at the dacha.

Now one of our sponsors for the Polar Ocean Challenge happened to be Johnny Walker whisky, and by lucky coincidence Sergei happened to have an appreciation for good Scotch. Two bottles of Scotch. Deal done!

This one evening with Sergei proved worth its weight in gold, for it was un-doubtedly his daily reports that allowed us to predict our course and navigate our way through the North East Passage. I also got a bonus, for as the evening at the dacha got chilly, Sergei presented me with a Russian immigration official's jacket that a colleague had somehow left behind, and which stood me in good stead for some of the arctic days ahead.

When we eventually reached Point Barrow, Alaska, with the last of the major sea ice behind us, I gathered together all the Russian money I could find on board, right down to the last rouble, and asked Nikolai to pass it on to Sergei with sincere thanks for helping get us through.

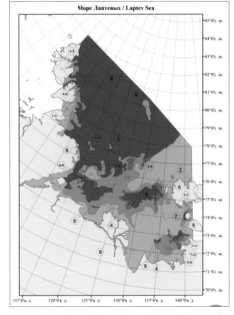

An example of an ice chart from the Russians, this one showing conditions in the Laptev Sea on 9 August 2016.

*　　　*　　　*

Murmansk was where we said goodbye to those intrepid mariners from the Thorn-bury Sailing Club – a farewell that was the subject of a 'survivors dinner' that I

Murmansk

Lenin, the world's first nuclear powered surface ship, now a tourist attraction in Murmansk. Built in 1957 her sole purpose was to keep sea routes open for cargo vessels along Russia's northern coast. It is a sobering thought that in sixty years, such is the rapidity of ice melt, powerful vessels like the Lenin *are becoming obsolete.*

hosted for them and for the crew that were to take *Northabout* on the second leg of the voyage, a smaller group comprising myself, Ben and Ros Edwards, Barbara Fitzpatrick, Constance Difede, Nikolai Litau as skipper and Denis Davydov as his first mate. With three Brits, an Irishwomen (Barbara), and American (Constance) and two Russians, we represented a pretty international crew.

Desperate to get underway, two difficulties immediately put a hold on my plans. First came the reports that the North East Passage was completely ice bound – solid ice right up to the land, the worst it had been for years – and, while the edge of the ice field was some ten days sailing from Murmansk, there was no point in forging ahead only to get stuck. Frustratingly, news then came that the North West Passage was now ice-free – weeks ahead of prediction.

The second problem was that our hard-won permit which we confidently waved in front of the immigration officials, was now declared to be the wrong one. The rules had changed and we would now need to call in to Providencia - a tiny administrative centre at the edge of the Bering Sea, opposite Alaska, to present ourselves and open and close a new permit, adding days to our schedule.

At least our enforced wait in Murmansk – with its 24 hours of daylight – was put to good use, with *Northabout* being spruced up. Barbara and Constance took off for St Petersburg while others satisfied themselves with a tour of icebreaker *Lenin*, now a tourist attraction permanently moored in Murmansk. Meanwhile Denis and Nikolai put their engineering skills to good use by fixing a couple of small problems with *Northabout's* engine.

I'd long learned that it's easy to underestimate the importance of food when undertaking lengthy expeditions such as ours. Food can be a great motivator, just as lack of it, or poor quality, be a demotivator. Only in extremis is eating emergency rations sustaining, and even that – when functioning as a team – quickly leads to fractiousness and grumbling. With Ros Edwards now on board, and having from the start been instrumental in devising a sail plan of what should be eaten aboard throughout the Polar Ocean Challenge, I was confident that this would not be an issue among *Northabout*'s crew.

Well before the expedition got underway, Ros had contacted all those intending to sail asking them to alert her to any dietary preferences or food allergies that would need to be considered. While few responded, Ros carefully made out a list of essentials from which a varied menu of meals could be prepared, taking into account *Northabout*'s relatively primitive galley facilities, the mixed culinary skills of the crew, and the watches aboard which made meal times very much a movable feast.

This meant that main meals followed a pattern during our passage through the polar oceans, each day a particular meal, with the pattern rotating over a week or more in order to provide variety while ensuring nutritional balance. A healthy quantity of non-essentials, biscuits and other snacks, topped up empty stomachs as and when required. And I swear, Ben could have eaten several pizzas and a couple of kilos of oranges at one sitting if he'd been allowed.

The installation of the microwave, also part of Ros' planning, was a stroke of genius, as was the breadmaker – for once the boat's circuitry had been rewired to cope with their demand, they made the preparation of hot, fresh food immeasurably easier and cut down considerably on the space needed for food storage.

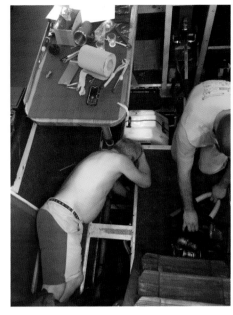

Nikolai and Denis make minor repairs to the engine while in Murmansk.

Ros had organised the food based around a rolling two-week menu. Constance and Barbara stocked up on fresh food in Murmansk so for the first week or so we didn't use the planned long-term food and had more variety, including fresh fruit and vegetables. We also had lots of eggs, some of which we stored under Ros' bunk and some in the keel box. A lot of the fresh food was kept in the cockpit and milk stored in the lazarette.

Ros Edwards' food planning took account of the somewhat spartan facilities aboard as this photo shows. Here Constance and Denis clean up after a spill in the galley.

I was somewhat taken aback to discover that even in the most remote places, there was always an opportunity to stock up on fresh food. Certainly in Murmansk, with its reputation for austerity and industrial grittiness, my illusions were somewhat shattered by discovering the supermarkets looked pretty much like those at home, clean, bright with shelves stocked with just about everything one could need – at cheaper prices.

Now, while I was more than happy to leave the victualling side of the voyage to an expert, I did draw the line at suggestions that we take a cappuccino maker, (I'd also banned the idea of a DVD player) and raised an eyebrow when I saw several varieties of tea bag arriving on board: fruit teas, camomile, earl grey and so on, luxuries that cut against the explorer grain. Yet I had to admit that your favourite cup of tea arriving after a day of stress gives a wonderful lift to flagging spirits.

One thing not accounted for was the Russian predilection for vodka and dried fish of which Nikolai and Denis appeared to have a never-ending supply. While we were never short, I was always conscious of the need to conserve food in case we should be ice-bound at any time.

*   *   *

Murmansk. Here, the 24-hours of daylight and the good weather offered plenty of opportunities to explore the city, although after almost a week waiting for favourable ice conditions, I was beginning to let my frustration show.

Nikolai checking ice and weather reports.

I'd noticed it before on other expeditions, as the time for departure draws near, a subdued and reflective atmosphere falls on the party as the risks and unknowns of the journey ahead are contemplated. This contrasts precisely with the palpable excitement that runs through the group towards the end of a successful expedition – relief and celebration mixed.

However, after almost a week stuck in Murmansk studying the daily ice reports that still showed the route ahead impassable, I was also aware how quickly the anticipation felt by the crew could turn to boredom and frustration.

Despite my respect for Nikolai's experience and judgement in sailing through arctic waters, I was beginning to feel that he was being over-cautious and that, without some positive motivation on my part, idleness would begin to get the better of us all. Attempting to persuade Nikolai to leave was a difficult decision for we could have no better skipper, yet I was beginning to realise that, while I had every reason to push ahead, Nikolai was quite content to eliminate all risk by staying put – after all he was being paid whatever – and I guessed he felt that making the passage in a single season over-ambitious on my part and that, consequently, overwintering was inevitable. So what's the rush?

Ros with her trusty Nikon, always at hand. Photo records of the voyage were vital, not only for our own family albums but for the daily updates on both the Polar Ocean Challenge and Wicked Weather Watch websites.

Barbara in Murmansk.

DAVID H-A'S BLOG
19 July 2016

With luck, and I have kissed my lucky beads, we will be off tomorrow. We are ready BUT whilst I am confident we will get through the ice, it is when and how. All of the Ice charts from Russia, Canada and the USA show we can get around across the Barents Sea across the Kara Sea and then we hit the ice. In ten days time will it have retreated enough? Could we get lucky and get a southerly wind for two days that would shift the ice off shore? Unknowns.

I am reminded of the quote in The Seven Pillars of Wisdom: 'All men dream, but not equally'. My dream is a long way from reality but at least we are bold enough as a team to try.

It is an interesting game of chess. If we leave until our path is free of ice, will we have enough time to get through the North West Passage before it re-freezes and get down the coast of Greenland and across the North Atlantic before the Winter storms chase us home.

So one step at a time. Leave and sail safely across one sea at a time.

On 19 July, after talking it over with Nikolai and Denis, it was agreed that we would weigh anchor the following day and head out for the North East Passage. If we met impassable ice, we'd harbour until the ice ahead cleared, or make plans for overwintering.

I'd made good use of the enforced wait by making sure everyone, including myself, was fully acquainted with the working of the vessel, particularly the emergency safety gear and the navigational and communication equipment. I held safety briefings with the crew ensuring that each was familiar with how things worked and capable of executing the necessary plans in the event of an emergency. We tested and retested all the running gear and ancillary equipment and, while this went on, Nikolai and Denis continued their work on the engine – the last thing we needed was any breakdowns in the ice.

This was more like it! *Northabout* was a hive of activity, everyone working with a will and a sense of joint purpose. Meanwhile, with the invaluable help of Raisa Kolosova in Frederik Paulsen's office, I was making sure that our permits were all in order and briefing the crew on immigration and customs procedures just to ensure there would be no last-minute glitches. While Russian bureaucracy was sometimes difficult to fathom, I'd learned that things worked smoothly as long as you'd ticked all the right boxes.

Against the background of Murmank's busy port, I carry out one of the safety briefings before we depart.

Nikolai explains to Barbara and myself the finer points of our Raymarine chart plotter and navigational display.

Below: Ros Edwards.

The afternoon of our departure Nikolai and I travel out to a small dacha on the outskirts of the city to meet up with his friends who had worked on icebreakers and were happy to share information with us concerning the passage ahead, and in particular the movement of ice.

What they impressed upon me was, that whatever the ice charts showed, the situation at sea could change rapidly. A southerly wind could blow the pack ice offshore leaving a seaway open that hours before had not existed. Their wisdom and confidence made me feel that all was ready for our adventure and I slept that night full of anticipation for our adventure to come.

*   *   *

ROS EDWARDS' BLOG
20 July 2016

The last week has been a whirlwind. I have been taking the North East Passage first week's food, and all of the baking and flavouring ingredients, out of the long term storage on the boat and putting them where we can reach them more easily while sailing.
So what will it be like? Will the ice clear to let us through in time for the subsequent legs to make it the whole way round in one season? Will the victualling be good enough that we can prepare what I have bought while sailing for 24 hours a day, even in rough weather, and everyone can eat well and stay happy and healthy – my responsibility and it feels huge.

The intended route of the second leg through the North East Passage (in red) and the actual route taken into the East Siberian Sea shown in yellow.

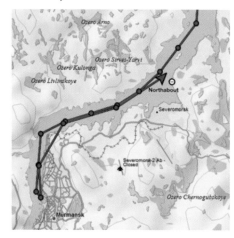

A screen grab from Northabout's boat tracker showing the narrow channel to be negotiated on leaving Murmansk.

Right: Nikolai and Denis on the day of departure from Murmansk.

On the evening of 19 July we ate together aboard *Northabout* and the Russian immigration people turned up as expected to check our permits and papers. I then remembered I was wearing the immigration officer's jacket Sergei had presented to me – quickly discarded to avoid confusion! A last minute problem in obtaining an open permit was overcome and with everything satisfactory an armed guard was put on *Northabout* until the moment of our departure.

Our voyage was to take us from Murmansk north-east into the Barents Sea to Novaya Zemlya where we would pass by that archipelago and then into the Kara Sea, the Laptev Sea and the East Siberian Sea, hugging the coast wherever possible and all the while hoping the ice has retreated towards the pole sufficiently to allow us passage.

We had hoped to leave early but it was late afternoon when *Northabout* slipped her moorings and began the passage through the relatively narrow channel which vessels have to negotiate on entering and leaving the port of Murmansk. As we didn't have pilot boat allocated to us, Nikolai was on the radio to the equivalent of our port authority or coast guard who kept an eye on us with radar, as we passed by the rusting hulks ice breakers and, further on, to where the Russian Mediterranean Fleet was anchored, a massive base to which we gave a wide berth. The fjord was as flat as a mirror; we sailed silently through beautiful scenery, not dissimilar to Norway, and while the moon had risen over one horizon the sun lay opposite her, attendant well-wishers for our journey into the fabled North East Passage.

*   *   *

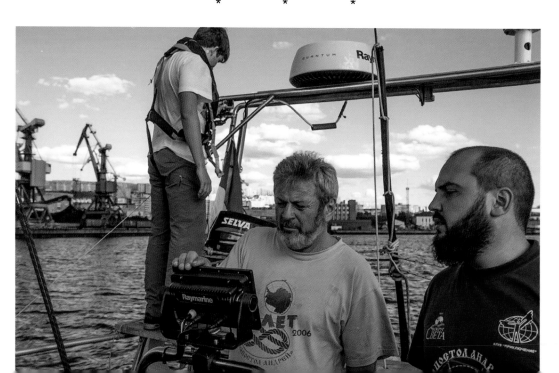

Ben and myself at the helm as we leave the land behind us and enter the Barents Sea.

DAVID H-A'S BLOG
21 July 2016

Into the Barents Sea. A slight swell, and a change in the colour of the sea to deep blue. The sun was still high and warm and Babs and Constance did a mean pasta with Bolognese sauce. Ros has thought of everything, and we must be the best equipped sailing vessel to leave these waters. We had three types of cheese to go with our pasta!

My watch is 8 to 12, first two hours with Ben and second 2 hours with Babs. And then our first sighting of a whale. No idea what type, but definitely a whale and not a submarine! And then I went to bed after a long, long day. It was too hot to sleep down below, and too many things going on in my head, but we are now on the North East Passage. Woooohooooo!

Nikolai and I had agreed that we would keep *Northabout* under sail for as much of the voyage as possible in order to conserve fuel for the engine should we be forced to motor when navigating through ice. Nikolai insisted that all the crew should be familiar with helming the vessel without the aid of the autopilot – a wise precaution in the event of an electronic failure and an important lesson in seamanship that, after all, was part and parcel of the purpose of the our voyage.

Looking ahead. An almost cloudless sky and calm sea as Northabout *heads into the Barents Sea – the calm before the storm.*

ROS EDWARDS' BLOG
23 July 2016

Yesterday was my birthday. After a normal day of watches, cooking and IT, the rest of the crew sprang a surprise – cakes, champagne and even bunting – and presents! The middle of the Barents Sea is a strange place for a birthday, but it will be unforgettable.

Pages from the watchkeeper's bridge log dated 24 July. We established good practice aboard Northabout *with hourly records of time, position, barometer reading, and general remarks etc. etc.*

This second leg was by far the longest of the four during the Polar Ocean Challenge and it was vital that we kept a daily log of miles covered against which we could calculate the distance our fuel reserves would take us should we need to motor rather than sail. So accurate were our daily reckonings of distance covered that by the time we reached half-distance it was possible to calculate, to the hour, our arrival at Point Barrow at the end of the second leg.

For the first few days *Northabout* flew along under sail and from 22–24 July we covered over 400 nautical miles across the Barents Sea. On our second day out, under blue clouds and across a turquoise sea, we'd celebrated Ros' birthday, and I could sense the crew were getting into their stride with everyone keenly taking up their allotted watches – and even the washing up rota was going to plan. However, our heavily laden vessel has a tendency to wallow in lumpy seas and those on galley duty are finding it a challenge - 'like cooking on a skateboard', comes Babs' complaint. Some of the crew are suffering from sea sickness as the weather begins to deteriorate.

Sun 24th July (5)

Time	Position	BAR	wind	cloud	SBS log	Eng Temp	Bar	VTW	BTW	log	Comments
01.00	74°49'.37N 050°40'.36E	1017	8.5	8/8	2476	off	12.	291	022m 5.5		PANda ON
02.00	74°52·16N 050°53'.89E	1017	8.4	8/8	2481	off	13.7	286	00in 4.3		PANda OFF
03.01	74°54.944N 051°07'.054E	1017	8.37	8/2	2485	off	12.	282	022m 3.8		Dolphins feeding - dozens & sunbros
04.00	74°57·549N 051°19'.391E	1017	8.35	8/2	2489	off	12.	278	022m 3.8		Start Engine
04.00	Sails strike off										
0500	75°00.5'N 51°33.4'E	1017	8.17	8/8	2494	ON	13.2	272	023 5.2		
					2500	ON	13.	267	023 5.2		
06.00	75°04.0 N 51°50.4	1017	8.3								
0800	75°10·4'N 052°22.3'E	1017	8.4	8/8	2510	ON	13.4	256	023 5.3		Lots of dolphins and a whale
0900	75°14·2N 052°41·8E	1017	8.4	7/8	2517	ON	13.5	250	023 5.1		Seals + Wood in the water.
1000	75°16.745N 052°53.59E	1017	8.48	4/8	2521	ON	13.6	247	016 5.2		Blue sky ☺
11.00	75°20·11N 053°10·11E	1017	8.3	3/8	2526	on	13.1	241	024 6.2		
1200	75°23·4N 053°25·3E	1017	8.1	3/8	2531	ON	13.9	236.	024 6.0		
13.00	75°26·63N 053°41·6E	1017	8.0	3/8	2536	ON	13.8	231.	023 6.00		
14.00	75°29.81N 053°59.01	1017	7.8	3/8.	2542	on	13.8	226	023 6.3		
15:00	75°32.61N 054°14.433E	1017	8.06	3/8	2546	ON	13.7	220	023 5.4		
1555	75°35.5'N 054°30.7'E	1017	7.69	8/8	2552	ON	13.4	215	024 5.4		
					2558	ON	13.1	209	024 5.5		
17.00	75°39.0 N 054°52'0 E	1017	7.43								Novaya Zemla in the distance
18.00	75°42'.19N 055°08'.7E	1016	8.06	8/8	2563	on	13.6	204	023 6.4		Pasta Puttanesca on the menu!
19.00	75°45'.32N 055°26.9E	1016	8.3	8/8	2569	on	13.5	199	023 6.4		Excellent dinner!
2000	75°48.4'N 055°45.1'E	1016	6.9	8/8	2574	ON	13.9	193	025 5.4		
2100	75°51·6N 056°04·0E	1015	7.0	8/8	2580	ON	13.5	187	025 5.5		
2200	75°54·48N 056°22·09E	1015	6.38	8/8	2585	ON	13.	183	024 5.3		
23.00	75°57.5N 056°41·2E	1015	6.2	8/8	2591	ON	13.6	177	024 6.5		Foggy.
	056°59.073E	1015	6.39	8/8	2596	ON	13.7	172	024° 5.6		

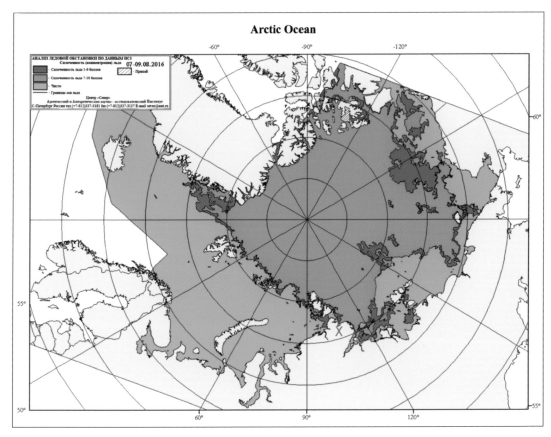

Arctic Ocean

Russian ice chart showing the extent of ice across our intended route through the North East Passage. The relative depth of the ice is shown in orange (polar ice) and green (sea ice) and at Cape Chelyuskin (marked with a red cross) the ice is impassable.

Still five days out from the ice, my own mood is not so upbeat after I check the daily ice charts and find our way remains blocked. While Novaya Zemlya is now in sight and the route across the Kara Sea free of ice, the chart shows that around Cape Chelyuskin and into the Laptev Sea the ice has not cleared. Nor is my temper improved by Nikolai explaining that this is unusual for this time of year and that the ice should have cleared by now! The final straw comes with Ben's practical joke with the smoke alarm – I am not a happy bunny!

The mood is not much lightened by the forecast which predicts heavy seas and strong winds. We agree that there's little point in attempting a rapid crossing of the Kara Sea only to then hang around waiting for the ice to clear at the cape, and so we continue under sail in order to conserve fuel.

By 26 July the weather changes as predicted. Blue seas and cloudless sky have given way to a uniform grey where the line drawn between sky and sea is indistinguishable. Temperatures have also fallen and the sea is choppy and short as we tack to and fro, making our way slowly east in the hope of finding a small, ice-free island where we can tie up and wait for the passage to open.

DAVID H-A'S BLOG
23 July 2016

Ben has a list of daily chores which he does diligently. The smoke alarm is situated over my bunk. Well yesterday I did 8 hours of watch solo, which actually is quite nice, as my partners were feeling under the weather. So I was ready for a long deep sleep. For the second morning in a row, members of the crew were witness to a 'dead to the world' big lump, sitting bolt upright in a millisecond after Ben accidentally pressed the test button. I was not a happy man!

I have not had a drink of alcohol since leaving Murmansk, except for a quick mouth wash on Ros' birthday. I think I must have the DT's! I thought it was a good idea to introduce a dry ship, except for Birthdays and the 7th rest day. Nikolai seems to have found his birthday is every day!

Early grump can only get better!

July 27 and grey seas under a grey sky as we sail slowly east waiting for a break in the ice.

DAVID H-A'S BLOG
27 July 2016

Couple of people off sick, weather again, sailing thrilling, choppy seas, but dangerous to do anything on deck or inside. Autopilot not working very well in these high seas, so all taking it in turns to helm. Safest place is in the bunk.

Two days of this now, but making some progress east, we think we might go into the middle of the depression, so calmer maybe tomorrow. We are then heading for an island for shelter and wait for new ice charts, regroup, sort out water maker. A problem but probably the low temp of water. 4 degrees. 8 degrees inside the saloon. Keel leaking a little. Ginger biscuits good. Luckily, I'm not suffering, and sleeping through the inside of a washing machine.

Nikolai and Denis did well today to cover for people. Clever bringing some Russians. Man they are hard, they think this is like a summer holiday!

If we hadn't known it before, by 28 July we were beginning to realise the serious nature of our adventure. Winds had increased to 7 or 8 on the Beaufort scale, gale force with attendant white-crested waves throwing spindrift and spray over *Northabout*'s reeling deck. No one ventured outside and the violent movement inside the boat prevented any sort of activity other than the essentials. Everyone was warned to wear their safety gear and clip on during watches, but with sickness it was often Denis or Nikolai who found themselves standing in for watches.

Here was a real test of our individual and collective responses and it was no surprise to me that all the crew came through with flying colours. The Russians seemed hardly to notice the violence of the storm and their calm efficiency had a settling effect on us all. But, seasickness apart, no one flinched from their alloted duties and no one suffered injury. Indeed it was me who nearly came to grief just as I was going on watch on the morning of the 28th.

I'd crawled out of bed, finding my sea legs under *Northabout*'s rocking and rolling, shivering as I got dressed and deciding to put my second thermals. After a quick check of the log I clipped on before leaving the saloon and again as I took over the helm, bracing myself behind the wheel. Sitting down, I put my leg up for stability just as a huge wave came across the boat. I hadn't seen its approach and was taken completely by surprise. For a fraction of a second, my whole body was under water, and it was only my leg stopping me going overboard.

As the wave cleared in a cascade of water racing over the side, I emerged with a mouthful of seawater, spouting like a goldfish in a Disney cartoon. Nikolai thought it was hilarious.

All over in a few seconds and no doubt my tether would have held had I gone completely overboard – but I'm very pleased it was me and not one of the lighter crew members.

Constance at the helm, clipped on and in full foul weather gear.

David was helming when the weather reached its peak. We approached a huge wave and as it filled the portholes' views the boat come crashing down. We braced for it to rock back up, it didn't. The swell was too high and we didn't go over. The wave came over the foredeck, the saloon, the cockpit. We're engulfed and for a second, the entire boat was consumed by the massive body of water. That second passed and the water roared off the decks as we plummeted into the trough on the other side. Water had come through in a dozen places: vents, the companionway and poorly sealed windows. But that was not my concern, I grabbed the cover of the companionway, pulled it back and breathed a sigh of relief. David was still there. Water would dry and we could place back any objects that had come loose but with a wave of that size the main danger was that David had been washed over while helming. True, I knew he was clipped in but all that really meant was that he could be being dragged behind the boat rather than be fully detached. As luck would have it he'd been positioned so that he was braced against such an assault.

The following day the wind has dropped and all hands put to work sorting out the damage and cleaning up inside. That night I'd been on watch and had taken the opportunity to start the Refleks heater (a clever little gadget that runs on diesel) in order to dry our wet weather gear. I'd urged everyone, the women on board particularly, to limit the use of the heater as it used precious diesel but my appeal had fallen on deaf ears. I swear, on some days you could have grown bananas in the saloon it was so hot! Eventually, we reached a consensus – the heater only goes on if the temperature drops below 8 degrees, although I suspect they turn it on while I'm asleep and off 30 minutes before I wake up!

Fortunately the storm did little serious damage, *Northabout* again displaying the quality of her original construction and refit. And every cloud has a silver lining, for we had hope that the wind may have driven the ice ahead of us offshore, leaving a passage for our way into the Laptev Sea. If not, we'd simply have to wait, finding a convenient anchorage where we could hole up until the ice relented.

Once more I found myself thinking 'what if' – what if the ice doesn't clear and we find ourselves running out of time, ice-bound and having to abandon the idea of making it through in a single season.

But my spirits were lifted by the news we'd clicked over another degree of longitude, reaching 80° – a crucial waymark I'd be dreaming out for weeks, although of course these longitudinal lines come pretty close together this far north.

Nikolai and Denis who began making bets on when our entry into the Laptev Sea would become ice free.

DAVID H-A'S BLOG
30 July 2016

We use a lot of power on board: chart plotter, radar, comms coming out of our ears, bread maker, water maker, In fact, we should have a small nuclear reactor on board. Anyway, we had this lovely brand new 'Panda' installed. Made in Germany. As we all know, tested to an inch of it's life and can work upside down etc. etc.. Except on the North East Passage... SO, this lovely shiny panda broke down. OMG! Panic on board. How would we cook our bread, send back emails and wash our teeth? So the Russians, Comrade Nikolai and Comrade Denis, they know one English swear word starting with F and a German swear word starting with S, and quite a lot of Russian swear words beginning with B. They have taught me well !! And these guys are extremely bright, probably both have electrical mechanical degrees in nuclear power technology. So, circuit diagrams come out, lots of F & S, lots more tweaks and spanners. Nothing. Dead as a Donkey!! F & S. Comrade Nikolai comes from the age of being a Khrushchev baby. Nothing was thrown away, you made it work. He built his car engine from scraps of baked bean cans. Anyway, he goes to the tool chest, comes back with a hammer. Taps something, BINGO!!!! The Panda started. Lots of F and German S and laughter.

Better weather also brought a change of mood in Nikolai and Denis. Where once I felt they would be quite happy to overwinter, I now found them avidly poring over our daily ice charts and making bets with each other as to when the passage would become ice free, Nikolai thinking it will be 9 August on his birthday, Denis by 6th, on his. The storms of the past week had indeed begun to shift the ice offshore, but whether sufficiently to clear the way we would not know until we reached the Vilkitsky (Vilkitskogo) Strait that lies off Cape Chelyuskin and forms the entrance to the Laptev Sea.

My relationship with these two had warmed considerably as we'd got to know one another, a friendship that was cemented in our little ritual, as the boat was closing down for the night, of sharing a glass of vodka and slice of herring or sausage – a Russian speciality of which they appeared to have endless supply.

*   *   *

We anchor in the lee of a small island group in a sheltered bay which the crew christen 'the Blue Lagoon', while Nikolai declares the place is called Wolf Cove. Here I take the opportunity of ribbing Nikolai by referring to a Russian scientific vessel that appears to be shadowing us as 'the KGB'.

The day before we spot our first ice – an unspectacular expanse but significant for us as it heralds the next stage of our voyage. This anchorage provides a perfect spot for us to regroup and prepare *Northabout* for our onward passage. The weather is fine and the sea calm, the first time the vessel's been on an even keel for days and the boat's alive with activity as everyone makes use of the calm that our brief respite allows. Brief, because the ice charts are showing significant movements ahead, with the storms having blown the ice offshore.

Above: *Our first sighting of ice.*

Northabout *enters The Blue Lagoon. Ahead is Pilota (Vasiliy) Makhotkino Island, named after a famous Soviet polar pilot, and part of the Nordenshel'da archipelago.*

It's not long after 8.00am and Barbara, Ros, myself, Ben (with his polar bear), Denis and Nikolai begin the day at our anchorage with me choosing the watches.

DAVID H-A'S BLOG
31 July 2016

This morning at our first anchorage and with everyone settled, then the luxuries came out. Mamont Vodka, supplied by my good friend Frederik Paulsen. I still can't slug a shot in one go, but slowly sip it, to the Russians' huge amusement!

The previous day, the 30th, I'd been on late watch and glimpsed mainland Russia away in the distance. On the seaward side one could also make out the markers for the Northern Sea Route, huge wooden structures, like lighthouses marking the way for seagoing merchant ships whose deep draughts keep them far out from the land. Here also were the remains of the first Soviet-era Polar Ice Stations that were strung out over this route. It is a sobering thought that, with future ice melt, we are likely to see millions of tons of shipping making its way through this fragile environment with the likelihood of pollution on a vastly increased scale. Allied to this will be nations fighting over the huge natural resources the region offers, with industrial development on an unprecedented scale. In a small way, it is my hope that the Polar Ocean Challenge will open the public's eyes to these changes.

Our sheltered bay was close to the point my friend Børge Ousland arrived at sixteen days out from Murmansk in his fragile trimaran *Northern Passage* – a voyage *Northabout* had completed in just eleven days. Bearing in mind the seas we had coped with, I reflected with admiration on Børge's gutsy expedition and wished I taken up the offer to go with him. Importantly, whereas Børge arrived on 16 August we were here on 31 July, in theory giving ourselves an additional two vital weeks to avoid getting ice bound.

The Northabout *laundrette.*

OPEN WATER — BREAKING ICE

But would the ice immediately ahead let us pass? We wait anxiously for each day's ice chart. As it is, the rigging of *Northabout* is now doubling as a washing line and our position is looking rather too domesticated for my liking. I want to get on.

We put the relatively balmy weather to good use: maintenance on the engine, chart plotter, generator and oven. Denis even indulges in a spot of fishing, without result, and Ben flies the drone, but overall the crew senses we are again in the arctic equivalent of the doldrums, waiting for a fair wind to allow us to get underway. While at anchor we can afford to change the watches, implementing an anchor watch for which each crew member is allotted a one and a half hour slot. This gave everyone a chance to catch up on much needed rest, particularly after the rigours of the storm which made all work aboard something of a trial and sound sleep almost impossible.

The anchor watches worked well up to the time when, in the early hours of the morning, a fresh wind drove ice into our little bay and gave those sleeping soundly a nasty wake-up call as it clanged against *Northabout*'s aluminium hull.

ROS EDWARDS' BLOG
23 July 2016

We are now waiting for today's ice charts with bated breath. We have enjoyed this little holiday but we are also keen to move on. I think we all have very mixed feelings – we are all chomping at the bit to get on with the expedition and try to achieve the goal of making it round in one season, but we are all very aware that we have several weeks of twenty-four hour sailing coming up, with the addition of sailing through ice which I imagine will often involve more people being on watch – to push the ice away and to spot ice from the bow, and using the drone to spot ice ahead of us.

BARBARA FITZPATRICK'S BLOG
2 August 2016

Whilst at anchor we have a respite from our normal watch routine and it is replaced with anchor watch, which is an hour and half slot, mine is from 12.30am to 2am. The other crew and Northabout are in a deep slumber, perfect quiet interspersed with gentle snoring from contented crew! Last night was an exception, as the wind picked up and changed direction, resulting in some bits of drifting ice coming into the bay, 'crashing' into the boat at about 4am, giving all the crew an alarming wake up call. There was no danger, it was simply the deafening noise of ice and aluminium in the still of the night! Denis was soon on the job with the ice poles, keeping all at bay!

Top: Northabout: *a drone's-eye view.*

Left: *Denis poling ice away from the hull.*

Denis was first on deck and began poling away the ice to stop it congregating around the anchor chain where its collective weight would begin to cause problems, possibly causing the anchor to drag, or perhaps worse to give polar bears easy access to the vessel – one can only imagine the chaos! This makes ice poles, around 15 metres in length, an essential bit of equipment when sailing in these waters.

But in some way these signs of drifting ice were good news, for if it was shifting here then it might also be opening the passage beyond the Vilkitsky Strait. The next ice chart would reveal if this was correct and we waited impatiently for news from Sergei.

We waited all day for our ice charts but, meanwhile, satellite photos sent from friends around the world revealed massive changes in just a few days and showed that we could probably get to the tip of the strait, after which there was just solid ice. It would probably take us a day's sailing as some of it would be through 4 to 6/10ths ice, some ice-free. I checked the forecast. It suggested a change in wind direction overnight that would drive the pack ice towards us as we sailed slowly up the coast. A glance at the map – no discernable shelter should we hit ice.

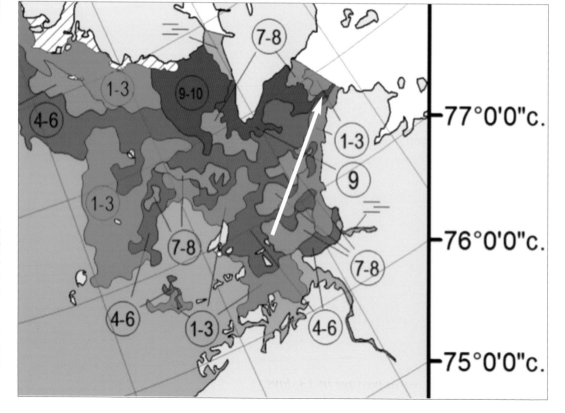

Ice chart of 5 August with our route from the 'Blue Lagoon' to the Vilkitsky Strait marked with a white arrow. The chart shows mixed ice ahead (the figures relating to the density of the ice, ranging from 9/10ths to 1/3rd) which offered a possible passage to the mouth of the Strait but no way beyond that. Our dilemma was whether to commit to sailing forward in the hope of taking advantage of a break in the ice allowing entry to the Laptev Sea – while knowing that there was no available shelter should we get stuck.

Our skipper, Nikolai. A great sailor, a fine companion, and a dab hand at repairing anything mechanical or electrical.

DAVID H-A'S BLOG
5 August 2016

Ros changed the anchor watch. We are from opposite ends of the spectrum. I am from the Richard Nixon camp, but Ros will tweak until perfect, which I admire, as long as it doesn't affect me! So last night I thought it was odd when Nikolai was going to bed at 9.30pm. On closer scrutiny, he was on anchor watch at 2.30 am. Russian captains normally do a floating watch, that applies to dish washing, anchor watch, cooking and sleeping. So off he slunk to bed. Don't mess with Yorkshire girls!

I hate indecision. Nikolai and I have talked for hours discussing the options – me inclined to push on, him more cautious. But bearing in mind the old adage about owning a dog and barking oneself, I listen to Nikolai. After all we do have time on our hands and it's better to be safe than sorry. So we are not leaving this anchorage just yet.

I think it's illuminating to include here, in Nikolai's own words (translated from the Russian), his account of sailing through these waters:

I've already done this route back in 1998–1999. Apostle Andrei [ocean-going yacht] and me were the first to do it in the history of yachting. We sailed from East to West, today we will be doing in the other direction, West to East. 1998–99 were very difficult in terms of the ice situation and therefore we had to spend a lot of time waiting for passages to open, and we even had to spend the winter in Tiksi because the trip could not be completed in one navigation season.

Since then the ice situation has substantially eased, because of the climate warming the amount of ice has decreased and yacht sailing became almost problem free.

An example to that was 2010 when Peter the Great yacht covered in one navigation season both Northern Passages and last year when a Chinese trimaran covered the whole North passage in 13 days.

Not gone yet? A seal visits while we sit and wait at the Blue Lagoon.

And our hopes for this year were based on these relatively simple ice conditions, but unfortunately when we arrived here this year, to the Laptev Sea specifically, it unexpectedly again got covered in ice and that hasn't happened in 10 years, this kind of ice conditions, so the task ahead is not that simple.

Now we are waiting for the Vilkitski Strait to open. Exactly 17 years ago I was waiting in the same archipelago, anchored, except after passing Vilkitski Strait, and before that we stayed in Laptev Sea waiting to be able to do it.

So the history repeats itself to some extent. And the task probably would not be easy. We will be waiting to see how the ice situation will be changing. We hope that passage will open and would allow us to pass this year both through the North East and North West Passages.

*   *   *

CONSTANCE DIFEDE'S BLOG
5 August 2016

Winter arrived. It has been four days since anyone has ventured beyond the cockpit to crush a can or add bits of rubbish to the lazarette. Occasionally the rain turns to slushy snow. It is 2°C outside with a Gale 6, gusting to 38 knots. The storm has peaked. The forecast is for calm winds by Sunday. If the forecast holds, we will have southerly winds on Tuesday. This is the most favourable wind to open up the ice. At least we are tucked into a sheltered cove. Who knew last Sunday we would be booking into a week's holiday on a Siberian archipelago. We continue to work through the fresh food from Murmansk. How many ways can you cook potatoes? Tomorrow we will have a party to celebrate Denis' birthday. Boiled potatoes, with herring and vodka.

It's 6th August and we're still, as it were, on ice. At least we have something to distract us from the waiting game for today it's Denis' birthday and we are all determined to celebrate it in style. Before getting too merry I check the forecast again and it looks like the predicted storm is on the way. If only it would shift that ice!

The weather in our little cove begins to deteriorate. As the wind increases Nikolai and Denis check the anchor winch.

After several vodkas Denis still manages to blow out the candles on his cake.

The day following we're all feeling a little worse for wear following Denis' birthday celebrations, except for Ben who is very enthusiastic about the idea of testing out *Northabout*'s tender. While we probably wouldn't envisage using it to go ashore until we reached Point Barrow, except in an emergency, it seems a good idea to me that we should try her out as she hadn't been in the water since the shake down cruise. Essentially carried as our ten-person liferaft, the tender took some assembling on the narrow foredeck, one of the outboards having to be unshackled from its bracket above the transom and carried forward to be attached. After some rummaging through the lazarette the paddles and fuel can are retrieved, all before the tender gets anywhere near the water.

Three people are then required to hoist the tender overboard, one heaving on a lanyard and two steadying the ungainly vessel, pushing it away from the hull as it's eventually lowered into the sea.

Ben and Nikolai are the first to have some fun, zigzagging about the bay, with Ben using the GoPro camera to capture shots of *Northabout* as they whizz past her. Then some bright spark suggested a group outing to the island and so everyone, except for Denis and I, climbed aboard the tender for a spot of sightseeing ashore.

DAVID H-A'S BLOG
6 August 2016

Denis's Birthday started off at 9am. Bunting up, card signed, cake baked. Phew! 'S dnem rozdenija'– which is Russian for Happy Birthday.
The ladies have had weeks to plan. Present of a tube map of London, a card, which looks like one I had when I was six, and a very nice red Mulberry leather note book – VERY NICE. I'm sure they bought it for me, but got mixed up.
So the lunch was boozy, It was Denis's washing up day, but as it was his birthday, the ladies voted I should do it for him, and then tried to use every utensil on the boat.
After a new siesta time, we are at dinner. Vodka time started at 6. They slug the vodka down in one, then they eat pickles, onions, cheese and biscuits. The next course is blinis with caviar and more vodka. Next course, hard boiled eggs , onions and vodka, then boiled potatoes and herring from Murmansk and vodka. Then a specially baked coffee and walnut birthday cake made by Ros, with vodka.
Even if we had clear waters, I think we are here for the night. One thing's for sure, we are running out of vodka, so we must be getting close to sailing!

Nikolai and Ben circling Northabout *in the tender.*

Nikolai, Barbara and Constance in the tender.

Constance, Barbara and Nikolai explore the island, Northabout *lying in the cove beyond.*

Northabout viewed from the tender.

Mother polar bear and her two cubs take a passing interest in the crew of Northabout's *tender.*

BEN EDWARDS' BLOG
7th August 2016

My Mother, Barbara and Constance got in and we went ashore. There's a shallow beach in the north of the bay we're in without any big rocks that we beached the tender on and got out of. We walked up and down the beach a little and then we all went up to a little cairn a few dozen metres up a hill, took a few pictures and then started walking back to the boat. Once we were back on the beach Mother looked over on to the other side of the bay and said, "That's a polar bear!"

My head snapped round to where she'd been looking and I saw three white dots not too far away moving in our direction.

I shouted "Bears!" a couple of times in case anyone hadn't noticed or needed any encouragement to get back to the tender and then ran along the beach followed by everyone else. Once in the water we were basically safe. The mother wouldn't want to leave her cubs and with the outboard we could move faster through the water than the bear could.

I suggested to Denis that this might be the time to break out the Beluga caviar and I was just about to take my first mouthful when, out of the corner of my eye, I caught a movement on the island. Where I half expected to see Nikolai and the gang walking along the shore, there was something altogether more alarming! A large female polar bear was padding along the shoreline with two cubs trotting along in her wake.

Luckily, the shore party had seen her too and were now making for the tender. A hungry bear is not to be trifled with, and though it was unlikely she'd leave her cubs, it was a good thing to see everyone back on board, even if it did spoil my and Denis' sneaky feast.

Denis and Nikolai manhandling the tender back on board.

Barbara.

If all this wasn't exciting enough, the following day we receive two great pieces of news. The first was that our permit had come through from Vladivostok allowing us to sail directly to Point Barrow without having to call in to have the permit closed, thus saving us at least two or three days. The second came via Sergei who thought that we would get a day or two of strong southerlies which might shift the ice away from the coast allowing us to slip through. But, he warned, this window of opportunity might only be open briefly and that we should sail closer to the mouth of the Vilkitsky Strait in order to be able to take advantage of it.

This is what I'd been waiting for. Nikolai ordered the tender to be stowed and the decks cleared and we were off. Even three of the crew immediately succumbing to seasickness did little to dampen my lifting spirits – though having three fewer hands to take watches meant it was going to be a long night.

*   *   *

DAVID H-A'S BLOG
7 August 2016

Winds calm and the first sun for a week. Exactly a week since we arrived. So we are waiting for some clear Sat photos of the ice. I have my own views on this, but best leave to a rainy day when I am in a better mood.

We thought it might be prudent to test the tender and engine before we reach Point Barrow. We don't want to be scratching our head a day out from Point Barrow on the open ocean. So huffing and puffing we managed to get it together. Engine fixed, a quick blast around the bay.

The end of a mixed day. First a walrus swimming around the boat, while Babs was singing happy birthday to her sister in Ireland, then the appearance of the polar bear.

So Babs says good things come in threes. Sisters 60th, walrus and a polar bear with two cubs is not a bad day. But she had better go and have a shower in holy water if we are going to get out of here.

Twenty-one days out of Murmansk and we are at last approaching the Vilkitsky Strait. The night we left our island anchorage we were met with strong winds with both air and sea temperature falling to just above freezing. As we crept slowly north we began to meet significant packs of 3/10ths ice and small bergs littering the sea's surface. On the distant coast we could just make out some of the old Russian markers and, beyond, the thin ribbon of land stretching down towards Cape Chelyuskin.

Old Russian waymark approaching the Chelyuskin Strait.

Ben at the helm.

While *Northabout*'s tough construction could withstand gentle collisions with drifting ice, it was important to avoid constant battering from larger chunks that were now dotted across our path. Sailing in these conditions was not an option and only motoring gave those at the helm the manoeuvrability they needed to steer a way through this floating obstacle course. Thankfully the wind had dropped which made this task a little less fraught.

Not being a crew who pass up an opportunity for a party, 10 August provided two good reasons, passing the Cape and celebrating Nikolai's birthday. Somehow Ben had managed to stash away a bottle of champagne given to him by our friend Margaret Gorley in Bristol who shared the same birthday as Nikolai, so out came the booze and yet another birthday cake ablaze with candles.

The Cape itself is the most northerly point of mainland Europe and Asia and the Russians maintain a polar station here, a scattering of wooden huts and a skyline bristling with antenna.

Happy birthday, skipper.

Distant view of the polar station at Cape Chelyuskin.

Russian tankers making their way through the ice.

As that day's ice charts came through we saw that any hope of proceeding beyond the Cape and through the Laptev Sea was thwarted by solid ice fields. Yet, we were on a roll, and even Nikolai agreed that it was worth sailing on to see how far we could make it. And if our luck held the southerly winds that were forecast might shift the ice away from the land enough to allow us passage.

We watched with envy convoy after convoy of merchant ships filing their way through the ice, way off shore, far beyond where we could venture, into what was the ocean-going equivalent of the M25.

So onwards we went only to find the ice rapidly closing in and forcing us to retrace our route back to comparative safety of an ice floe held fast against the shore of Volodarsky Island where we anchored overnight. Next morning we woke to find ourselves surrounded in all directions by a massive pan of ice which threatened to hem us in. Only by a huge effort poling backwards and forwards did Nikolai, Denis and I finally release *Northabout* from her icy prison.

I hate retreating but we had no choice. The current ice maps showed 10/10ths ice ahead and with a storm forecast it would be madness to rely on our floating ice-island as a haven. First we tried edging down the coast – impossible. Our only option, to backtrack on our previous night's course while Nikolai and I studied the ice charts and weather forecasts in the vain hope of magicking a way through. Ros at the helm played her part that night by weaving her way through 3/10ths ice for 30 miles in an attempt to reach the coast, but to no avail as the ice fields became thicker and thicker – and so another retreat.

Barbara helming her way through the ice.

ROS EDWARDS' BLOG
11 August 2016

A stamukha is an iceberg that is touching the bottom. We had to turn round from the ice by the coast last night and find somewhere safe to moor/anchor. There were strong winds so we needed to find somewhere else to sit them out, and the answer was a stamukha against which we moored, knowing that it would drift. Ben came to wake me just after he had taken over on watch and said he wasn't happy, we had drifted too far, and I agreed that we should wake Nikolai. Nikolai was not happy with the situation and said it was right for Ben to wake him, we had drifted a long way, and he detached us from the iceberg and we helmed back. We were heading back to the area where we had moored to the iceberg to find another one, to repeat the floating mooring when Nikolai and Denis spotted a stamukha. This made an excellent mooring. Later, the wind shifted and we needed to move round the stamukha to provide shelter because we were now exposed. When we did this, we discovered a Northabout-shaped harbour on the other side (see the picture on the opposite page) which provided fantastic shelter.

Three times we nosed our way forward, three times *Northabout* turned her head about to seek out a safe anchorage among the small island group at the entrance to the Laptev Sea. With little sleep, I was beginning to feel the strain and, after a dinner of lentils that night (I hate lentils!) the midnight toast was to 'clear waters'.

August 11 and awake at 8.00am to find a steady wind blowing from the south. After phone calls with Sergei, Nikolai and I agreed there was the possibility of the ice being driven offshore, although the ice charts showed little actual change ahead. The choice was stay, or go, and our collective pioneering spirit soon saw us underway.

I had the first helm, and that depressingly took us north to get around a large solid strip of ice, but once through this, it got easier during the day. The team were great, and all pleased to be making slow progress along the coast. Genoa in and out, engine off and on, rain off and on, reflex on and off. We'd sailed 12 meandering miles and tied up that night alongside a stamukha grounded near the coast.

At the stamukha, with Barbara and Constance looking very happy to have found some shelter.

The next morning nature again dashed our hopes, and as the ice began to converge around us, in order to avoid its clutches, we had to move closer to the coast, even lifting the retractable keel to give *Northabout* the shallowest possible draught.

Edging our way forward we passed the junkyard remains of a former Soviet polar station, all the while weaving in and out of the ice, shuffling backwards and forwards in some kind of odd nautical dance. Ahead we could see the tall marker on the island Ostrov Andrei beyond which we knew there was open water but those three miles might just have well been three hundred.

The wind was too strong for using the drone to spot possible leads ahead and so Denis climbed to the masthead and, from this precarious perch, directed the helm. Again Nikolai and I discussed our options and, with the wind picking up and the sea state deteriorating, it was becoming clear that we'd have to find shelter – and quickly! As later described, what hit us was hurricane force winds averaging around 65 knots and at one point, almost unprecedented for this region, gusts reaching 78 knots. Certainly the worst storm we encountered on our arctic legs.

The thought of retracing our 11 hour course back over 40 miles was almost unthinkable, not least in the amount of fuel that would take. Then a large floe came into sight which would offer temporary shelter and we gingerly approached it, tying up alongside this natural vast pontoon.

But pontoons don't move and this one was being driven along by the wind at 1.3 knots. Being far too dangerous to remain, we untied and headed again for a large stamukha where we anchored for the night.

New ice charts did nothing to lift our spirits, in fact they were worse than the last ones, and now we had a massive storm coming our way – 35 knot winds with gusts of 50 predicted. At least this should break the ice up. My sleepless nights have also gone into sleepless days. One thing for sure, I can understand why the Russians drink so much !

*   *   *

August 13, unlucky for some, and for us if we don't find shelter. After nudging along the coast we eventually sneak into a narrow estuary and wait out the storm. Earlier, with Denis up the mast again, we eventually found ourselves passing Ostrov Andrei, an island which had previously seemed well out of reach. First thing today the water had been perfectly calm, like a mirror, and just as well for we found ourselves in shallow water, measuring 0.2 metres on the depth meter, and at one point grounding.

Amazingly, as the storm approached, so the air temperature rose, at one point reaching 17° – and in a moment never to be forgotten, as the wind freshened it brought with it the faint smell of burning, from forest fires some five hundred miles inland.

Denis up the mast shouting directions.

CONSTANCE DIFEDE'S BLOG
13 August 2016

For this moment in time, we have solved the puzzle. The labyrinth of ice which has trapped us for days is consigned to the past. It was a team effort. Denis, at the top of the mast, for more than an hour, called out directions to Captain Nikolai, who has taken over the helm from Barbara, with her Irish good luck finding the leads. For the first time since we left Murmansk, all of the crew is on deck. The sea is flat, wind calm, the light magical and we are electrified by our new found freedom. The forecast for tomorrow is a Gale 8, but that's for tomorrow.

Northabout *sheltering beyond Ostrov Severnyi for two nights 14-15th August, to see out the storm.*

Northabout

The storm when it came was one of the worst I have ever experienced in arctic waters. It doesn't matter where you are in the world, in a tent, or a boat, it can be scary to find yourself at the mercy of mother nature. Because *Northabout* is so tall, she catches the wind and this, combined with the shallow water in which she was lying, where the waves are even more exaggerated, put tremendous strain on the anchor and chain. Thank God for Nikolai's experience. At the height of the storm he was with Denis helming towards the anchor, very slowly with the motor ticking over. I have never been taught this technique, or even read about it, but it saved the anchor.

Meanwhile, I called everyone into the saloon for safety's sake and it was only after midnight that the winds started to abate. At times like this you think the worst. Does it build character? I'm sure it does, but I can think of easier ways to do it. One thing for sure, the team were great, and we will drink for years to come of that night. I gave Comrade Nikolai my vodka for the first toast – he'd certainly earned it.

The Laptev Sea did all; she could to keep us close to her bosom. Although we were now covering serious miles, between 17 and 19 August we continued to meet with large areas of ice and individual bergs but, as we entered the East Siberian Sea, on 20 August, a new menace now appeared – fog.

At the height of the storm, all the crew don their survival suits and gather in the saloon.

DAVID H-A'S BLOG
17 August 2016

Last night was a bit of a panic. We might run out of Vodka, wine and scotch, but also OMG! toilet roll. With a captive audience, I showed everyone what I was taught on Everest by the Sherpas. Just use one piece of toilet paper per poo. Well, you would have thought I had just shot Constance between the eyes. Her facial expression was such, she was just about to throw up, her cast iron stomach had not succumbed to sea sickness, my little trick nearly did it! Well luckily, our supremo Provisions Director Ros, did a quick count, and luckily found we had enough for two squares per person, so panic over.

Russian ice chart for 18-19th August showing the East Siberian Sea. On the far left of the chart are the New Siberian Islands which guard the entrance from the Laptev Sea. On the far right is Wrangel Island, the approach to which is shielded by the remnants of the melting ice which obliges us to sail further south and thus take a longer route.

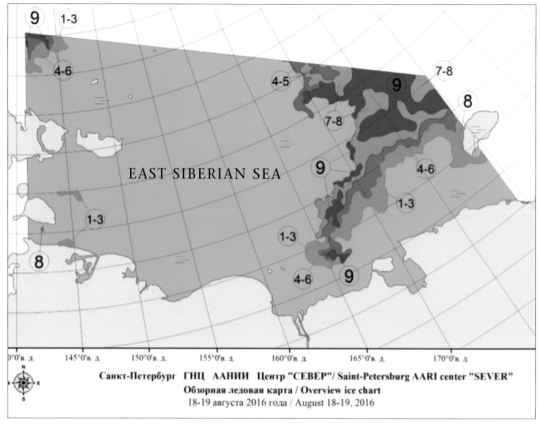

The ill-fated USS Jeanette.

DAVID H-A'S BLOG
21 August 2016

Well after the scare of last night, the boys did a full service on the engine and oil change. Changed filters, swopped tanks, had their last shot of Vodka and started the engine. Fingers crossed again, but engine sounds sweet. If we didn't have the engine we would have done just a few miles. Genoa up now and giving us some distance. Whilst making progress, our East is slowing down. Our course it's not straight East now, but South East. We are going a lot further South than predicted, as we have a large tongue of ice coming down to the Coast. The only way around sadly is South, hopefully that is all it will take to get through. Our last ice of the East Siberian Sea.

These two perils slow our progress and yet we are still making good miles each day. On 21 August we pass the New Siberian Islands, sight of one of the great stories of polar exploration, a tale to rival Franklin's tragic expedition. Here the USS *Jeanette*, a naval exploration vessel under the command of George De Long, became trapped in the ice for two years from 1879–81, was released and trapped again, finally sinking 300 miles of the Siberian coast. The fate of De Long and his crew is a gripping tale of determination and courage, well worth reading.

Just as the rhythm begins to return to life on board *Northabout* after surviving the turmoil of the heavy ice, the engine starts playing up, suddenly revving and then slowing to its usual steady beat. Each time it happens my heart leaps to my throat and I have visions of being out here with only sail to rely on. Nor do I relish the thought of having to make for the Russian coast for to do so means having to give 48 hours notice, 24 hours, and finally 8 hours notice of where you intend to enter Russian waters and where you intend to exit. Red tape I'd like avoid like the plague. Once again our Russian comrades come to our aid and with their mechanical genius soon have the engine running sweetly.

August 22 was a confusing day as Nikolai decided to change the clock and put it six hours forward. A sensible idea as we were still working to Murmansk time, but as we're still operating the same watches confusion reigns!

On my early watch I was greeted by the phenomenon known as 'Fata Morgana' – a strange atmospheric distortion that makes objects on the horizon appear vast, and early mariners were confused by what they thought were great walls of ice, or massive waterfalls blocking their route.

Then at sunset we were treated to an amazing display of the aurora borealis which brought all the crew on deck to witness a truly amazing sight.

That evening the new ice charts showed how right we were right to come south, and now just skirting the southern edge of the ice. They also revealed just how lucky we'd been to clear the Laptev Sea when we did, for now much of the passage we'd made it through was now closed. For us, if our luck holds, it'll be a straight line run to Point Barrow.

On 24 August, after skirting more floating ice, the charts show us to be finally clear and I raise a glass to our friend Sergei without whom we should almost certainly have found ourselves overwintering. His provision of ice and weather data had been critical to our success.

CONSTANCE DIFEDE'S BLOG
23 August 2016

Oh what a night!! Just when you might think we have seen it all, the celestial bodies have come together to reveal an out-of-this-world spectacular. The sunset has given us an alpenglow, for hours on end, with the deepest of oranges, pinks and purples streaking across the sky. The sky is filled with friendly dragons, eel, fruit loops. A three-quarter moon has risen through the mackerel clouds, shining its light on a mirror of silver sea. It is so flat you could waterski, were it not for the bits of berg scattered about. We are ice helming, by moonlight, in a fantasy land. It is a time of indescribable beauty. Laughing with delight, we pinch ourselves to be sure our eyes do not deceive us. And just when we though it could not get any better, the aurora borealis appeared, spinning in the form of a pinwheel across the sky, with Venus shining as its crown jewel. We are privileged to witness this magical kingdom.

Denis' photo of the Aurora Borelais.

On this day we also passed the 5000 mile mark after leaving Bristol and now have sailed so far south that the mountains on the mainland, the highest since Murmansk, stand out clearly on the horizon. We are also just passing the Russian port of Pevek and approaching Wrangel Island between which to places lie the straits passing into the Chukchi Sea. On an earlier trip, while on a scientific expedition with Frederik Paulsen, I had landed on Wrangel Island, said to be the last place the hairy mammoth roamed – and now with melting ice revealing more and more of their remains.

For two days we battle against contrary winds and choppy seas which makes life on board difficult, especially sleeping when you can be fast asleep one minute and suddenly wake up in mid air.

DAVID H-A'S BLOG
25 August 2016

Today we had a head wind, so slow going. Getting to the edge of the world is proving tiresome. With our new watch times, people disorientated. We change another two hours at midnight tonight. We could see the mainland for some time, then it slowly disappeared. Slowly, slowly.

A lot more small birds flying over the sea at the moment. Our track to get the best wind is towards the ice, and north-east, hoping this will change during the night, and bring us back south to our waypoint.

Constance, Nikolai, Denis and me celebrating crossing with 180° line of longitude with a sip of Johnny Walker.

Then comes the great moment as we cross the 180° line of longitude, the exact point on the earth opposite Greenwich and from now on we're on our way home!

Our celebratory supplies of drink ran out some time back but we've saved the last drops of Johnny Walker whisky to salute this moment. On this leg, we have passed through the Barents Sea, Kara Sea, Laptev Sea, into the East Siberian Sea and now the Chukchi Sea. We are due more high winds but our waypoint is now straight for Point Barrow, just 400 nautical miles distant.

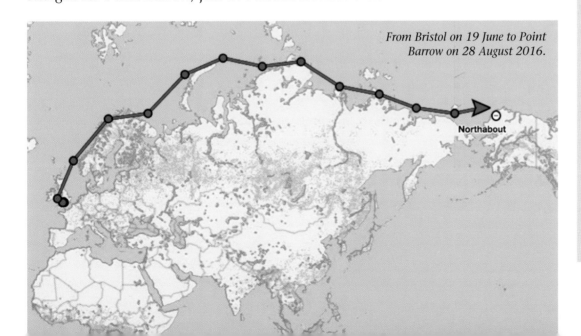

From Bristol on 19 June to Point Barrow on 28 August 2016.

Northabout

ROS EDWARDS' BLOG
27 August 2016

The Chukchi Sea is wild and we are wet, tired and hungry. We are into the second day of 25 to 30 knot winds, throwing the boat around and everything in it. Many people are feeling queasy and not managing to eat very much. We are being thrown around in the saloon whenever we try to do anything, such as make a cup of tea or cook dinner. I for one feel ill, weak (through not eating enough), and slightly sick all of the time. All of our kit is soaked from being washed over when we are on watch. We can't light the stove to dry things out or warm up because it doesn't work when we're heeled over. Nikolai has himself strapped into his bunk with bungees to sleep. David is not sleeping because his ley cloth is not keeping him in his bunk properly. Apart from that we are having a wild ride.

95

DAVID H-A'S BLOG
28 August 2016

So the last couple of days in the Chukchi Sea. In a rolling sea, it is difficult to stay in your bunk let alone sleep, so everyone is a little grouchy. So what is this like… ?

Well, how do you do your number ones in such a sea state of rolling waves and 25 knot winds. Well our toilet, 'Heads' have a little bowl, with a hand pump. Ladies it's easy, they just sit. Well the boys its harder, firstly you have to find your John Thomas through several layers and get him lined up. Meanwhile because of the pitching and rolling, you have to stand 45 degrees to the bowl, and hope the toilet seat doesn't chop your crown jewels off.

Number twos. Oh my goodness! You have to plan this one… Firstly, hold on to the wall handle, or boat, or you are a goner. Sit down, and try and do your business. Holding on to the wall handle for dear life. DON'T let go. with your other hand find the paper: 2 sheets rationed only! Holding on to the wall handle. Tear off two sheets with your teeth, with your other hand try and wipe your delicate bottom, then try and pump the handle to get rid of your breakfast. To put this into context, its like riding a bucking bronco, whilst trying to do the essentials.

Our 'heads' have a flimsy plywood door, more than once I have head butted the door while sitting on the throne. Actually, its quite dangerous, I wonder if we did a risk assessment for that one?

Well, well, it's 28 August and we passed the date line and the W 168 58.620 at 16.57 boat time, that is the point at which we can inform the Russian authorities that we have finished their Northern Sea Route, and we no longer have to report to them daily. We will celebrate this milestone when we get to Point Barrow. It's only just sinking in what we have all done.

Thank goodness for Dima and Raisa who'd organised our Russian permits, avoiding the need for *Northabout* to call in to Providencia in order to have the permits opened and closed, thus saving us at least ten days – precious time that would otherwise certainly have found us overwintering.

And finally a nice touch from the Russian coastguard signalling 'Good Luck!'.

Third Leg – The North West Passage

"At the turn of tide we perceived that we were being carried, together with the pack, back to the eastward; every moment our velocity was increased, and presently we were dismayed at seeing grounded ice near us, but were very quickly swept past it at the rate of nearly six miles an hour, though within 200 yards of the rocks, and of instant destruction! As soon as we possibly could, we got clear of the packed ice, and left it to be wildly hurled about by various whirlpools and rushes of the tide, until finally carried out into Brentford Bay. The ice-masses were large, and dashed violently against each other, and the rocks lay at some distance off the southern shore; we had a fortunate escape from such dangerous company."

Perils of the North West Passage – from *The Fate of Sir John Franklin* by Captain F. L. M'clintock, published in 1869

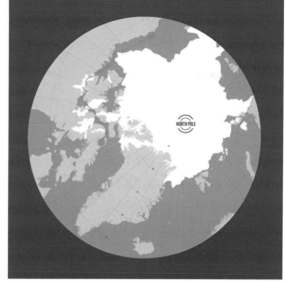

The route of Northabout*'s third leg.*

As so often happens, following the elation of success comes the descent back to earth and the realisation that normal life goes on. For *Northabout* and her crew this meant buckling down to make passage across the Beaufort Sea at the start of the next stage of our voyage – the North West Passage. And make no mistake, while the ice melt has given sailing in these waters more certainty, they still hold many of the perils encountered by Captain M'clintock and his crew.

Our immediate problem was facing a steady 15 knot wind dead on our nose, which made the crossing to Point Barrow hard sailing. Overnight on 29 August Denis and Barbara shared the onerous duty of steering through heavy swell and lots of ice that, to add to their difficulties, had not appeared on either the Russian or Canadian ice charts. And it was not until the following morning, when I came on watch, that the grey ribbon of land came into sight – Point Barrow, Alaska.

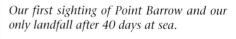

Our first sighting of Point Barrow and our only landfall after 40 days at sea.

As we slid into a small lagoon I silently thanked Jarlath Cunnane and those who took so much care in building a vessel that had survived two crossing of the North East Passage – the first small boat to have done so from both directions. *Northabout*'s Irish roots gave additional significance to having Barbara aboard, the first woman from that country to conquer the Passage. As for Ben, the youngest person to have made the North East Passage on a small sailing vessel, he could take full credit for playing a significant role in our success – proving himself to be mature well beyond his years.

As for myself, I took some quiet satisfaction in having achieved what many doubted could be done, and in doing so while maintaining a harmonious crew aboard our little boat despite all that the arctic elements could throw at us.

*　　　*　　　*

Point Barrow was the departure point for Ros and Denis, their places on board to be taken by Ros' husband (and Ben's father), Steve, and our new first mate Johan Petersen, a Norwegian who had previously sailed through the North West Passage. While these transfers were going on, the crew enjoyed the somewhat spartan offerings that Barrow had to offer. Sadly, I missed out on joining in the fun as I didn't have the same visa as the rest of the crew, having flown in to pick up the boat in Murmansk, and was in danger of arrest should I venture ashore.

DAVID H-A'S BLOG
29 August 2016

We have made it! And there are so many people to thank: Cheryl Lingard, Nick Martin and Nikki Webster have spent two years of their lives organising the trip so far. Frederik Paulsen, Raisa Kolosova, all the incredible help from Sovfracht company, especially Chairman of the Board, Dmitry Purim, General Director of the Sovfracht East Aleksandr Khrustalev, and Ivan Okorokov, who is the head of maritime in the Sovfracht.
And last, but not least, my incredible crew mates who survived in each others company for 40 days. We did it. When Ros left the boat in Point Barrow to go home, I promised her a lovely cup of tea in England. And our able Comrade Denis who also left the boat in Point Barrow; I promised him a Vodka in Moscow.

Ben, whose skill and endurance belied his years.

But as I've said before, the people who live in these remote parts of the world have a warmth and sense of shared responsibility from which more 'civilised' communities could learn a lot. Here we were offered every assistance and the crew and I enjoyed our brief respite here which gave us time to restore some order aboard *Northabout* and to restock and refuel, this last costing and arm and a leg with diesel at seven dollars a gallon, amounting to a bill of almost $500. It also gave us brief time to reacquaint Steve with the boat and to introduce Johan to his new crewmates and, while it was sad to say goodbye to our shipmates Ros and Denis, the changes had a reinvigorating effect too. Not least for those who found our handsome new Viking crewman of particular interest!

Twenty-four hours and we are at sea once again, the next stop along the North West passage being Tuktoyaktuk a remote Inuvialuit hamlet located in the Inuvik Region of Canada's Northwest Territories, 500 nautical miles distant. This will be the first place we've been allowed to dispose of the accumulated rubbish aboard and where we can replenish fuel and water, do the laundry and have a shower.

The weather forecast is not good, with the troublesome headwinds persisting along the coast and, just as I was thinking how much Steve can enjoy this leg without constantly dealing with bilges or sorting out the comms, the auto-pilot decides to quit.

Scenes from Point Barrow.

99

Ice map showing concentrations of ice around Point Barrow as we approached on 29 August. Our route took us along the coast towards Demarcation Point, although contrary winds meant slow progress.

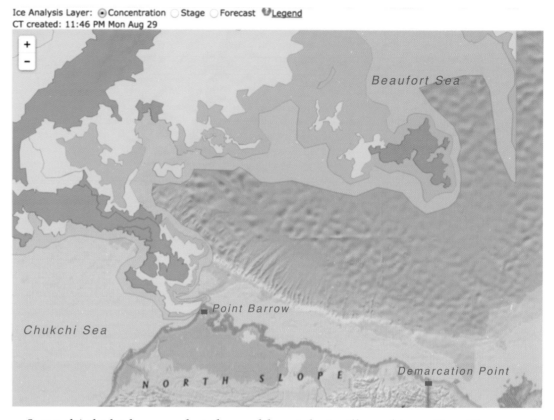

Ice Analysis Layer: ● Concentration ○ Stage ○ Forecast ⬦ Legend
CT created: 11:46 PM Mon Aug 29

Beaufort Sea

Chukchi Sea

■ *Point Barrow*

Demarcation Point

N O R T H   S L O P E   ■

DAVID H-A'S BLOG
1 September 2016

Well, my Comrade Cpt Nikolai and I have had an amusing day seeing the two ladies float around our new Viking Navigator crew member, like bees around a honey pot. Ooh Johan, we keep the milk here. Oooh Johan, would you like a cup of tea. Well at one point Johan was just showing us on a map where he had sailed in Antarctica. Ooooh Johan really, ooooh Johan you're so brave, Johan did you get cold? At which point Comrade Nikolai had clearly had enough. Big Dog (Nikolai) comes over from the chart table: "When I circumnavigated Antarctica it was so cold, we used Ice cubes in our sleeping bag to warm us up. I never wear gloves, that's for little girls. When I got to Australia, I wrestled with an alligator to keep fit..."
At which point, Nikolai goes back to his chart table. You could see loyalties were torn. When our Viking said he was going to get some sleep before his watch, a little Irish voice sang out, nite nite Johan, sweet dreams! At which point Big Dog just laughed.

Steve thinks he knows what the problem is but will need to wait until we reach Tuk in order to fix it. This means we're back to helming which in heavy seas with a headwind becomes a real chore, especially as an eye has to be kept out for ice. We try motoring while the wind remains against us and hope the forecast is right that lighter winds are on the way.

I keep it to myself but I'm relieved that from now on, if we do get ice bound, at least we'll be able to overwinter on either US or Canadian soil, making life so much easier from the standpoint of visas. Once in Canadian waters we are told to make daily contact with the Canadian customs people – who turned out to be extremely accommodating when it transpired Nikolai had the wrong visa.

A day out from Point Barrow and the terribly sad news reaches me that my friend and former teacher, Mansel James, has died. This is a moment for reflection as almost certainly, without his encouragement and guidance, I would not have taken on the many adventures that filled my life, including the Polar Ocean Challenge.

The following day, 1 September, dawns dull and grey but the wind has died and the sea is less choppy. Eventually, as we pass Demarcation Point, which marks the

New crew – Steve and Johan.

border between the USA and Canada, the sea calms and the sun breaks through, leaving us with a most glorious day. As the sun sets we were given a free display of amazing sun dogs (haloes around the sun caused by refracted ice crystals) and in the distance we could see the snow-capped mountains of Herschel Island which lies off the Yukon coast.

BEN EDWARDS' BLOG
1 September 2016

Something that is very good is the addition of a certain Norwegian to the boat. While Denis was nice and very good at the sailing we couldn't really talk to him and this made life a little, not much, but a little, difficult. Johan on the other hand can speak very good English, is also a very good sailor and very nice to be around. He's got the attitude that I've come to associate with very tough: very confident with just a hint of silliness to their humour. It's a good combo.

Constance, Barbara and myself planning ahead.

Entering the harbour at Tuktoyaktuk in the evening gloom on 2 September.

DAVID H-A'S BLOG
2 September 2016

Rick was the Oracle of everything this trip is about. He was born in Tuk, and has gradually seen the climate change. Summers earlier by a month and winters later by a month, resulting in a huge change of lifestyle for the hunters in this area. Fascinating and absolutely terrifying change in such a short time.

It's day 46 out of Murmansk and on the evening of 2 September *Northabout* is steered through the buoys marking the channel into Tuktoyaktuk harbour. The lights of the town are twinkling as we tie up alongside a pontoon (it's noticeable from now on how we're leaving behind the long arctic daylight hours), to be greeted by Rick, the man with the keys to the local fuel tanker.

Refuelling, I should point out, had been preying on my mind ever since leaving Barrow. There we'd decided to top up only until we reached Tuk where the fuel was so much cheaper. However, we'd also learned that we'd be arriving on Labour Day – a national holiday which our tanker man would be spending on a fishing trip. This would mean our hanging around in Tuk for four days, time we could not spare, unless I could persuade Rick's man to delay his holiday. As ever, that pioneering 'can do' attitude came to the fore and, with the enticement of paying up front (with a tip for the driver too) we were directed to a new pontoon moored directly beside the tanker.

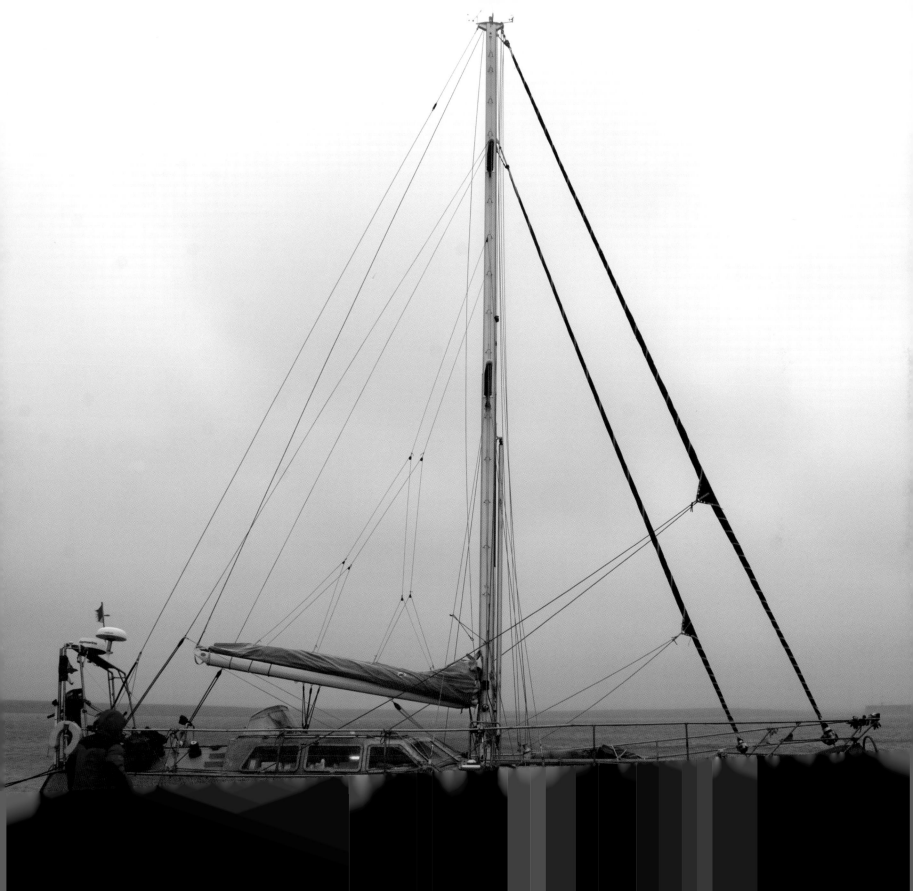

Northabout being refuelled from Mr Gruben's tanker in Tuktoyaktuk. Our little boat had taken some pounding in the days before our arrival and here was a vital few hours of opportunity to refit and refurbish her.

DAVID H-A'S BLOG
2 September 2016

Doug the local Big Boss came to check up on us, he soon made us aware that there were no Taxis, Hotels, Restaurants, pizza parlours, nothing. So we send Mrs Irish (Barbara) off with him with Comrade Nikolai to look at another possible pontoon. So, they come back. Poor Doug had been poleaxed by Mrs Irish. We had his truck free of charge for the weekend. Oh, and his Boss' house to use, with shower and laundry and he will come and sort out our engineering problem in the mornings. We could use his company pontoon for the night. So a great day, and finished on a high, of spare ribs.

Tuktoyaktuk will be familiar to TV addicts as the place at the end of the line in the reality series 'Icetruckers', based on the lives of the men and women who deliver fuel, food and equipment to the mines and oilfields of Alaska and Canada. But Rick's accounts of how things are rapidly changing here in the far north are in themselves chilling and, if global warming is a portent of things to come, then the traditional life of the indigenous people, the environment and its wildlife, is about to disappear forever. Coupled to these changes will come exploitation of onshore mineral resources, while offshore giant tankers will ply their way throughout the year through ice-free seas.

Inuvialuit residents of Tuktoyaktuk. These happy and generous people are facing disastrous changes to their traditional way of life and their environment. While we may not slow the progress of the planet warming, we can at least prepare our world for the enormous changes ahead. My hope is that, in a small way, the Polar Ocean Challenge will help direct our thinking towards the future.

Myself, Nikolai and Johan outside the Boss' house.

Willard Craig. He and Steve spent hours in the workshop making a new spigot for the broken autopilot. I could see that Steve was in his absolute element, working alongside Willard to create what was a precision bit of engineering completely from scratch. The look of satisfaction on Steve's face when he'd fitted the new part in the confines of the ship's bowels – and it worked – was a real picture!

The 3rd September gave everyone an opportunity to recoup and refocus. Use of the Boss' house gave everyone an opportunity to watch a little TV, shower and generally spruce themselves up. Afterwards each of the crew is handed a jobs list with such essentials as checking ice lights, bilge pumps, doing the laundry and shopping – Tuck has two supermarkets! Here we could also clear the mountain of rubbish from *Northabout* and, with the newly created space, rearrange the accommodation onboard.

Steve meanwhile had been dropped off at the workshop of Willard Craig whose generosity was prevailed upon to help repair the broken spigot of our autopilot. These two men shared an engineering genius that kept them at work all day in a freezing container that doubled at Willard's machine shop. Using the original broken parts as a template and working to fine tolerances they made a completely new spigot which then had to be fitted in the bowels of the Lazerette in cold weather and driving rain. It worked first time. Brilliant!

Once again, these people, living at the ends of the earth in conditions where daily life can draw on the limits of human endurance, turned their hand to help complete strangers – always prepared to put themselves out for others.

*   *   *

Spare ribs for supper.

Tracking chart 5 September, Northabout having passed Cape Bathurst and heading towards Amundsen Gulf.

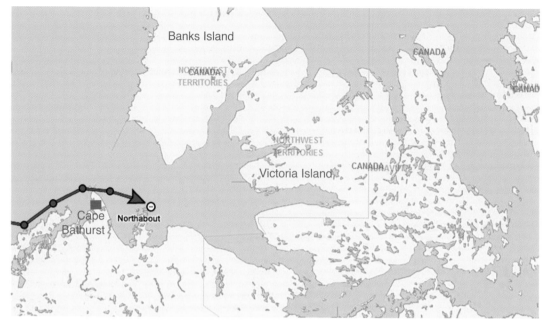

DAVID H-A'S BLOG
4 September 2016

Tuk was a great tonic, and the place and people had been kind to us. What a great feeling to have a clean body and clean clothes. My underwear was getting whiffy. I use Norwegian wool underpants. Rune Gjeldnes taught me, you wear them one way for 20 days, then turn them inside out for another 20. Problem was I was up to day 45!!

Leaving Tuktoyaktuk.

We left a cold and damp Tuk at 8.00am this morning, making our way slowly in light winds back along our inward track. *Northabout* heads east along the Tuktoyaktuk shelf where you can normally see bowhead whales, but all we saw was great baulks of floating timber washing out to sea from the Mackenzie Delta which meant those on watch had to react pretty quickly to avoid some pretty big logs. Thankfully the autopilot is working like a dream.

Johan Petersen relaxing as Northabout *heads goose-winged into the Amundsen Sound.*

106

From now until we reach Upernavik at the end of this leg we're passing through waters and past islands whose names resound with characters from history – those early explorers who came to the region in search of the fabled North West Passage. It's very exciting to see history rolling out in front of us, every cape, bay and headland named after someone significant.

In good seas and with a following wind we have sailed 169 nautical miles in the 24 hours since leaving Tuk, a huge contrast to the hard yards gained against the headwinds in the Beaufort Sea. Johan allows *Northabout* to show us the best of her sailing qualities by setting the sails goose-winged – poled out either side of the main mast – and sending her scudding along at 9 knots. Jarlath would be proud of the old girl! However, from the Canadian ice charts it's apparent that our intended 'short cut' through the Prince of Wales Strait is impassable due to

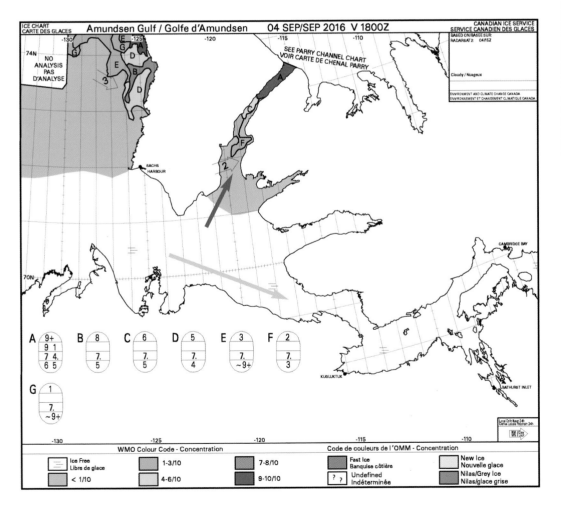

BEN EDWARDS' BLOG
5 September 2016

We left Tuk yesterday. So far we've been very lucky, we've had following winds ever since we left and have been doing over seven knots most of the time. We're at one hundred and twenty six degrees at the moment, when we reach one hundred and twenty we'll be two thirds of the way round. Exciting prospect, we're almost done. In light of the lack of ice and in the spirit of saving time we've decided not to stop in Cambridge Bay or Pond Inlet and go straight on to Upernavik in Greenland before doing our crew change. Looking at the ice maps at the moment it seems we'll be able to get through with little or no trouble, though this is almost bound to change, if it stays that way we'll reach Upernavik in about fourteen days. I'm looking forward to it!

As we've gone east over the past two days things have been getting much colder remarkably quickly. The water temperature has dropped by five degrees and though I'm not sure of the numbers for the air temperature it certainly feels a lot colder.

Canadian ice chart for 4 September. The Prince of Wales Strait (blue arrow) is blocked by ice and Northabout's *passage is via the longer but ice free Amundsen Gulf (green arrow).*

A view over the stern as Northabout *races before the wind through the Amundsen Gulf.*

DAVID H-A'S BLOG
7 September 2016

A mixed day. My first watch this morning at 8am was delightful, no wind, so sails down and calm waters. Progressing past various islands in the Coronation Gulf, lovely passing the coastline and making distance.

On my watch this evening, it's a proper winter's evening as we move slowly into Dease Strait, the wind has returned, but smack on the nose. I also think the wind is being funnelled through this narrow strait, creating a very choppy sea. Our speed has halved, which is miserable.

The magnetic compass is dancing all over the place and totally useless here. Getting the influence of the magnetic pole.

Ben and me on watch as we sail through the Coronation Gulf.

the extent of multi-year ice and this means we will have to take a more southerly course through to Cambridge Bay. And so, *Northabout* is headed towards the relatively ice free Amundsen Gulf, the channel that runs between Victoria Island and the mainland.

Cambridge Bay, farther on, is a crucial waymark for, should we meet ice that threatens to block our progress, it represents the last refuge for overwintering. And should we meet ice once we've passed that point we would need to be certain that we can retreat to Cambridge Bay as a safe haven.

As if to reinforce the need to be vigilant (and fortunate!) as to our prospects of success through the North West Passage, the Russian ice charts come in that night and reveal just howl ucky we had been in getting through the North East Passage. The charts show that whilst beyond the Laptev Sea there is clear water, in the Laptev Sea itself the ice has returned right up to the coast blocking any route through it. Had not the storm arrived when it did to temporarily push the ice offshore, we woul have been forced to overwinter.

On 6th and 7th we continue to make good progress and push on through the Dolphin and Union Strait (named after the two small boats used by the naturalist John Richardson who explored here in 1864) towards Coronation Gulf. What I find interesting is the almost complete absence of freighter traffic here, whereas in the North East Passage we encountered a steady stream of shipping. Odd considering the North West Passage is shorter and subject to less red tape.

STEVE EDWARDS' BLOG
8 September 2016

Beautiful skies all day, different colours, with sun occasionally on the land. You really do feel the history and presence of the past here.

Tonight (8th September) we passed Turnagain Point, named by Franklin as the furthest East on his first overland expedition of 1819–21. On their return journey from this expedition the explorers suffered great hardship and starvation, surviving on lichen and ultimately eating their boots, after which Franklin became known throughout England as 'The man who ate his boots'.

As a young boy scout I was told to always trust my compass when navigating. That advice is good as long as you are in the UK, however in the North West Passage we are close to the magnetic North Pole and this has two effects. Firstly the North Pole magnetically is much closer than the real or "true" North Pole, so we are going past it quite quickly and therefore the direction of apparent North is changing quite quickly. Secondly the earth's magnetic field is usually about horizontal and compasses are built assuming that this is the case. However when you are so close to the pole the magnetic field is mostly vertical as the field disappears into the ground to join up with the South Pole field in the centre of the earth. This means that not only are magnetic compasses quite unreliable in the NW Passage but that the errors can vary enormously from compass to compass depending on the details of how they are built.

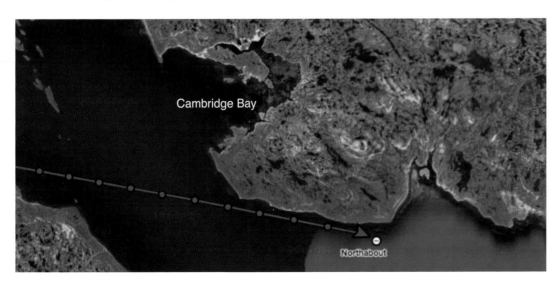

Our track past Cambridge Bay and into Queen Maud Gulf.

Later, with the wind at our face, we make slow progress along Dease Strait, past Cambridge Bay and into Queen Maud Gulf, very much feeling this was our 'point of no return'. With Cambridge Bay receding over our stern and the ice charts showing open water all the way up to the Bellot Strait (the narrow channel that separates Somerset Island from the Boothia Peninsula), for the first time I allowed myself to hope that our Polar Ocean Challenge would be successful. Even the wind appeared to be turning in our favour with the expectation that we could use sail all the way up to the Bellot Strait. Yet the forecast also showed the possibility of ice closing in and I was under no illusion that the luck we'd enjoyed in the North East Passage needed to hold.

The following day we have one of those chance encounters at sea that have a touch of serendipity about them. In the middle of a bleak arctic sea a small vessel hoves into view off our port side, grey hulled with yellow upperworks, looking for all the world like a lost lifeboat. This was David Scott Cowper and his son

STEVE EDWARDS' BLOG
8 September 2016

Johan has written a book on knots, sadly in Norwegian. It looks very good and we are pressing him to have it translated into English. Knowing about the book several crew members have asked for knot training and the photo is of Barbara being shown a highwayman's hitch, or in Norway a smuggler's hitch. The point of this knot is that one rope is quite secure but can be released very quickly by pulling on the other rope. It was widely used by highwaymen for tying horses and by Norwegian smugglers.

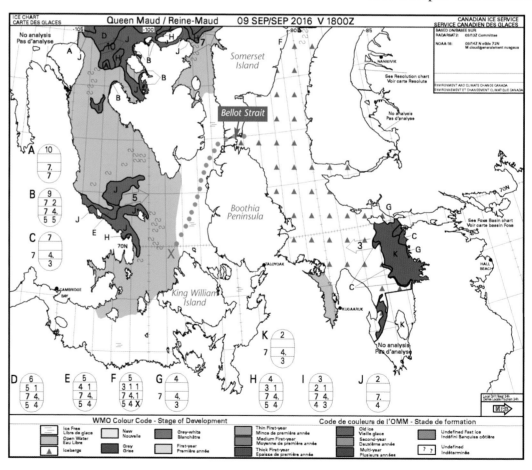

Canadian ice chart (with location names added here) for the area around Queen Maud Gulf for 9 September. The red 'X' shows the approximate position of Northabout *and the green track is the route taken up to the treacherous Bellot Strait and into the Gulf of Boothia. The red triangles represent the presence of icebergs.*

David Scott Cowper's Polar Bound *on her way through the North West Passage.*

Freddie aboard *Polar Bound,* on their way through the North West Passage via the Fury and Hecla Strait. I'd known about their intended route but to come within sight of each other was a truly surreal experience, two sailors chatting away over the radio in one of the world's most remote places. A legend in high latitude sailing, David was heading into Cambridge Bay for breakfast and invited us to join him but, sadly, with the prospect of ice and storms forecast, we had to decline. As we parted company each sailing our own path through that immense seascape I couldn't help thinking about 'Mad Dogs and Englishmen'!

*   *   *

This is indeed a god-forsaken place if the elements turn against you and one's thoughts turned again to Franklin and his crew held fast in the remorseless ice. It was about here, off King William Island in 1846, that Franklin abandoned his vessels and here, 170 years later, the remains of HMS *Erebus* (in 2014) and HMS *Terror* (2016) were discovered by underwater archaeologists. Almost to the day, as we sailed close by King William Island, the world's press announced that the wreck of HMS *Terror* had been found lying in remarkable condition on the sea bed, her ship's bell being recovered and brought to the surface.

With all these placenames reminding one of the fate of so many explorers who had gone before, coupled with the grey skies and greyer seas, this region draws on itself a cloak of sadness and despair – a gloom that the continuing head wind aboard *Northabout* does little to dispel.

*   *   *

BEN EDWARDS' BLOG
9 September 2016

In the meantime we've been moving along and came across the only other boat we've seen in the North West Passage. About sixty foot long and obviously built for very tough conditions we passed the motor yacht Polar Bound on its way to Antarctica. Sounds odd but apparently they're going through the North West Passage the other way and are then going to go down the Pacific to Antarctica. Good luck.
According to the very affable man we talked to over the radio a place we have to go through called the Bellot Strait was very clear when he was there. The Bellot Strait cuts hundreds of miles off our journey, is about eighteen miles long and only a couple of miles wide. I hope we can get through.

A diver shines a light on the ship's bell of HMS Terror, *discovered at 24 metres depth in eastern Queen Maud Gulf.*

Johan playing his movie role from 'Titanic' as Northabout *enters the Bellot Strait.*

DAVID H-A'S BLOG
11 September 2016

One of the best days of the trip. I got up for my watch this morning, no wind, and the sea was calm. A sprinkling of snow on the nearby hills. We were heading for the elusive Bellot Strait. After reading so much about it, it was a big milestone. The Irish found it blocked with ice and couldn't go through it and our good friends Børge and Thorleif had trouble with packed ice in the channel.
As we approached, I think everyone was apprehensive. Everyone wanted to be on deck. The Bellot didn't disappoint.

Throughout the trip, Ben picked up, was given or found, various good luck charms which he attached to the bow rail. They obviously worked, for we sailed through the Bellot Strait in the calmest of seas, completely free of ice.

The Bellot Strait is a treacherous narrow passage of water about 2 kilometres wide and 25 in length, flanked either side with barren cliffs. It's named after Joseph René Bellot, a Frenchman who was Captain William Kennedy's navigator when they searched for Franklin back in 1851. Ice allowing, it will lead us eventually into the Prince Regent Inlet, the Lancaster Sound and Baffin Bay. It's important to get the tides right for our passage in the strait as they rip through at up to 12 knots and any floating ice could do nasty things to a boat's hull.

There was thick ice when Børge Ousland came through in *Northern Passage* in 2010, and Jarlath in *Northabout* found the route blocked. But we had more immediate problems when we approach the strait as the magnetic compass is going haywire and the autopilot seems equally confused. I recall that Amundsen experienced the same compass problems 100 years back. To add to our worries the ice chart for the days ahead showed ice building up in the Prince Regent Inlet.

The end of our passage through the truly magnificent Bellot Strait.

For now, though, conditions could not be more idyllic. We had zero wind, so the surface was like a mirror and the steep cliffs and hills reminded me of Scotland. We had worked out the best time for a transit from the tide tables and at one point we reached an impressive 11.9 knots. Throughout the passage we all stayed on deck, transfixed by the raw beauty of this special place. At the end of the strait we slowly edged past the famous Magpie Rock, the foot of which roils with turbulence as the tide flows around it.

But, beautiful as it was, I couldn't stop myself thinking about what this ice-free channel represented in global terms – a part of the world that up to very recent times was pretty much ice-locked – indeed had not been transited until the late 1940s. And now we didn't see one piece of proper ice, not even a floating ice cube for a G & T. What this means to these wild places in the future, the effects on its wildlife and indigenous peoples is almost beyond imagining.

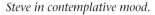

Steve in contemplative mood.

Barbara, Constance and I don our Explorers Club headgear to celebrate our passage through the Bellot Strait. Founded in New York City in 1904, the Club promotes the scientific exploration of land, sea, air, and space by supporting research and education in the physical, natural and biological sciences.

BEN EDWARDS' BLOG
9 September 2016

We're through the Bellot Strait! It's an almost completely straight passage between two islands lasting eighteen miles and cutting a huge section off the journey. It almost always has ice in it but as we went through today it was completely clear. It's odd, hundreds of people died trying to find the North West Passage. Caught by ice and storms they either froze or were shipwrecked. And we went through seeing a grand total of seven small floating ice chunks. If I hadn't already been through the North East Passage I might wonder what all the fuss was about. A grim testament to greenhouse gases.

After exiting the strait we made our way into a little bay at Fort Ross sitting at the southern tip of Somerset Island. Here are two historic little huts that were owned by the Hudson Bay Company and now maintained by the Canadian Coast Guard. Above the huts is a cairn that was built by Captain M'clintock during his search for Franklin and, by happy coincidence, it was his great grandson John M'clintock who performed the naming ceremony of *Northabout* – this very boat that Jarlath built and which has performed so magnificently for both expeditions.

From Bellot we entered Prince Regent Inlet and here we came to our first ice, as forecast, although now so thick that it threatened to seal off the strait. If we didn't get through, then it would be a long slog back to Cambridge Bay to overwinter. The ice has changed rapidly in the last few days, thickening and closing the route at the top of Prince Regent Inlet and also to Resolute Bay – winter is on its way.

We plodded on for an hour attempting to find a way through 5/10ths ice, too thick for us to go through although we could see clear water on the far side of the floe. Barbara came on watch and by an amazing piece of helming managed to squeeze *Northabout* between two pans of ice and into open water. Her skill at this point almost certainly meant the difference between reaching Greenland or backtracking with our tail between our legs all the way back to Cambridge Bay for overwintering.

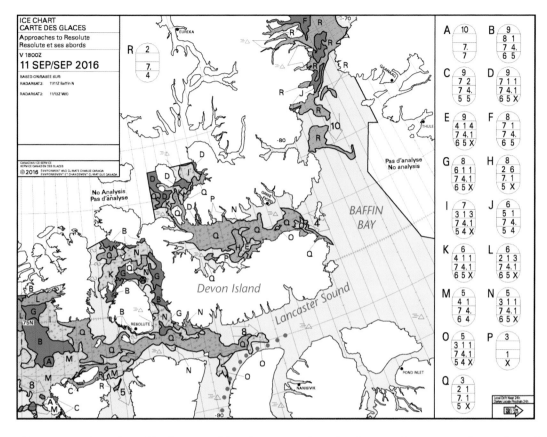

ICE CHART
CARTE DES GLACES
Approaches to Resolute
Resolute et ses abords
V 1800Z
11 SEP/SEP 2016
BASED ON/BASÉE SUR:
RADARSAT2: 11/11Z Baffin N
RADARSAT2: 11/13Z W/O

CANADIAN ICE SERVICE
SERVICE CANADIEN DES GLACES
©2016 ENVIRONMENT AND CLIMATE CHANGE CANADA
ENVIRONNEMENT ET CHANGEMENT CLIMATIQUE CANADA

No Analysis
Pas d'analyse

EUREKA

BAFFIN BAY

Devon Island

Lancaster Sound

RESOLUTE

NANISIVIK

POND INLET

THULE

Pas d'analyse
No analysis

The Canadian ice chart for 11 September showing the extent of ice as we are about to enter Lancaster Sound from Prince Regent Inlet en route for Baffin Bay – our approximate track inserted in red. To the west, Resolute Bay and the Barrow Strait are already choked by the encroaching new ice.

Even so, there's still plenty of broken ice ahead of us in Lancaster Sound and in the pitch dark trying to avoid lumps of ice the size of a car is exhausting. The bigger bits you can see on the radar but the concentration you need is intense. It's like driving down the motorway next to a lorry in the rain, you can't see a thing but hope you get to the other side when the wipers have cleared the screen. Horrible!

Spotting ice.

BEN EDWARDS' BLOG
12 September 2016

Ice! just when we thought it was all over. For the past day we've had the wind and tide behind us, we've been doing nine knots at times. So of course, right at the end of my watch we come into thickish ice just as it's getting dark. The next six hours were tricky. Weaving in and out, trying to find a route and occasionally gently nudging pieces out the way. I do however have a new candidate for scariest moment of the trip. It was the last half hour of my watch. We were going at nine point two knots over the ground and it was getting dark enough that seeing was getting tricky. We'd seen some pieces of ice earlier and so were looking out and has the radar on screen. I was sitting on the plank at the back of the boat and saw a wave breaking about thirty meters off the bow. I then noticed that the white on the water wasn't going away, I grabbed the torch we keep up there and turned it on, there was a large piece of ice twenty five meters off the bow that we were heading for at nine knots. I jumped down to the wheel, hit the standby button and yanked the wheel sideways. The boat swerved quite wildly and we missed it by ten meters or so but I noticed I was now jumping at every breaking wave I could see.

Lying in my bunk that night my fitful sleep was accompanied by an orchestra of crunching ice hitting the hull and the complaining beat of the engine, forward and reverse, manoeuvring around the ice.

We later devised a system where one person would be at the helm and one at the bow with the torch. The helmsman would then, with luck, see the ice as the torch was swung on to it and do their best to not hit it.

But over all what a day! I have gone from thinking of overwintering in Canada with the boat, to now getting to Greenland as planned.

*　　　*　　　*

Leaving Lancaster Sound for Baffin Bay.

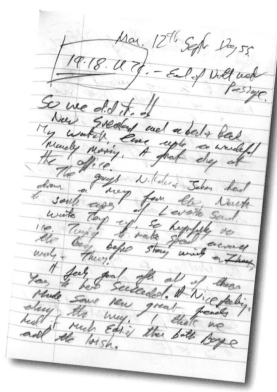

We Did It! Page from my log book of 12 September 2016.

Well after a horrid night of avoiding ice using torches to pick out the larger pieces, the next morning broke bright and clear, the ice completely cleared. The mountains either side of Lancaster sound, coated with new snow, stood like welcoming sentinels, their glaciers flowing down to the water's edge.

We are now on our way across Baffin Bay. We exited Lancaster Sound, the entrance for the North West Passage, on 12 September. Had we really done it? Three long years of planning and dreaming. Three long years of sweat, blood and tears. And now we had crossed the line.

But, and there is always a but, we have to beat a storm to Greenland. The water temperature has gone up to 3.4. so probably no ice in the water, but we have the radar on to spot the big icebergs in these waters. It's pitch black outside and the watches are lonely and cold. No stars, both the main, genoa and steel mast on to make swift progress. The last weather report showed 40 knots near Greenland, so still a great adventure. But I will sleep with a smile on my face tonight.

We are now well into Baffin Bay, trying to outrun some high winds. I think we should get some tasty weather in the morning, but I'm looking forward to seeing the mountains of Greenland, hopefully by tomorrow afternoon. The latest ice charts show a huge amount of 9/10ths old ice has blocked Lancaster Sound and Prince Regent Inlet. It looks like we got through by the skin of our teeth.

The 15th September is a slog of a day across the choppy seas of Baffin Bay, probably the worst conditions we've endured since our traverse of the Chuckchi Sea. But gradually the headwinds relented and the sea swell grew less, as if nature itself had finally given us her blessing on our success.

We sight a few icebergs on the radar and during the day pass close to one that resembles the rock of Gibraltar, a huge lump of ice. The currents take them from the glaciers of Greenland up the coast, hence the region being christened 'iceberg alley'.

*   *   *

So this is my last watch. We're out of vodka for our usual midnight toast, but I think my comrade has found some cooking rum with which to salute the new day, and hopefully the village of Upernavik in the morning.

Final Leg – Greenland and Home

It is 5.00am and Johan, who is on watch, has woken me as we approach tiny Upernavik harbour. It's hardly light yet and as we sail towards the coast of Greenland we pass silently among vast icebergs looming out of the semi darkness. It is an unforgettable moment.

It is the 15 September and my part in this epic voyage is almost over. Any sense of regret at leaving *Northabout* is overwhelmed by a sense of achievement – both a personal satisfaction and for those who had shared this journey with me. Mission accomplished!

Two days earlier, I'd been faced with a dilemma as to whether to follow the original plan of landing at Pond Inlet on Baffin Island before entering the immensity of Baffin Bay. Here Barbara, Constance and I were scheduled to leave the boat in order to take a flight to Greenland and home. However, the forecast predicted a heavy storm coming in over Baffin Bay and the idea of leaving *Northabout* shorthanded for the crossing was quickly dispelled, thus we made a bee line for Upernavik.

DAVID H-A'S BLOG
15 September 2016

A slog of a day across choppy seas of Baffin Bay. Not as bad as other rough seas we have had, but we are so close to a nice beer, that the yacht doesn't want to get there before closing time! You have to be so careful in these seas. Always holding on. Poor Constance who is built like a whippet, had wet hands coming off watch, got into the saloon and lost grip. She crashed through the door of one of the bunks and took the door of its hinges !!
Three people felt sea sick, and one was gracious to be sick outside, that's after being hardened by some pretty nasty weather on the way, so just shows what it was like.
I have been blessed with no sea sickness from day one. Partly because I never take my wrist seabands off. I have no idea how they work or in fact if it's just psychological but it has worked for me.

Calm before the storm, entering Baffin Bay. The hours of endless daylight were now behind us and we were having to get used to sailing with only starlight above us.

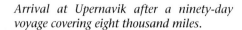

Arrival at Upernavik after a ninety-day voyage covering eight thousand miles.

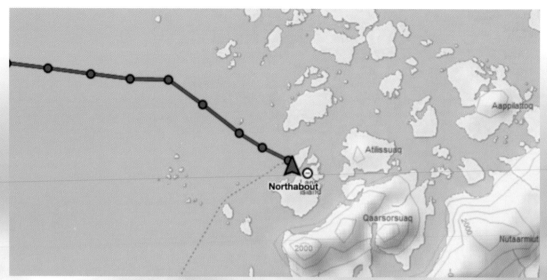

The prospect of enduring yet another storm after our successful transit of the North West Passage, and this time with the added danger of icebergs, left the whole crew on edge but our luck held and, while the wind and waves did their best to make life uncomfortable, this was kids' stuff compared to earlier experiences. In the middle of the gale, on my watch, I recall seeing the lights of a Chinese fishing vessel rising and falling as she fought her way through the heavy seas, so far from home.

As we progressed south, so the long arctic days were giving way to hours of darkness and here in Baffin Bay we were treated to the spectacle of starlit skies and the magic of the magnificent aurora. Later, the lights of Upernavik hove into view as we edged towards the coast on a bright morning that heralded my last day at sea on *Northabout*.

We glide into the still sleeping harbour and tie up among the fishing boats. Here we will meet up with the new crew who are to take *Northabout* on her final leg back home. While the others leave to spend their first night on land for some time, Nikolai and I stay on board, along with a bottle of vodka – a last, rather sombre, celebration in which we toast each other's part in this epic enterprise.

*   *   *

Upernavik.

The following day Barbara, Constance and I are already in the air as the new arrivals Ros, Colin Walker and his wife Alison, and Frances Gard (a photographer and film maker specialising in 'green' projects) are collected from the airport ahead of a celebratory reunion dinner with the remaining crew. Ros has even brought a lasagne in her rucksack for Ben, all the way from England.

BEN EDWARDS' BLOG
15 September 2016

It's over! We're in Upernavik! A total of ninety days, eight thousand and forty one miles and we are now the first British boat to have done the North West and East Passages in one season! Things have been difficult at times, seasickness, having to be tidy and a teenager, but it was without a doubt worth it. Baffin Bay was horrid. Headwinds all the way and the worst swell we've had since the Chuckchi Sea. The last twelve hours have been steadily better. The swell slowly got smaller and I finally saw the Northern Lights, true they were kind of sad and pathetic but they counted. The last hour into Upernavik was amazing. Huge icebergs everywhere and islands in-between. Just before we tied up Johan fished a piece of ice out of the water for our celebratory coke or vodka (depends how old you are).

Here's me looking like a vagrant having borrowed a shopping trolley to move my gear from Northabout *as I head for home.*

The North West Passage crew aboard Northabout *shortly after we arrived in Upernavik on 15 September. From left: Ben Edwards, Steve Edwards, Johan Petersen, Constance Difede, Barbara Fitzpatrick, myself and Nikolai Litau.*

BEN EDWARDS' BLOG
16 September 2016

Upernavik is an odd place. It's a very small town built on a hillside. All the houses have half of themselves up on stilts so they're not leaned over. Because of the angle there aren't any normal streets, instead they've got winding roads that somehow manage to go past every house. The small harbour they have is inside a bay with a number of large and really quite impressive icebergs. There's no real pontoon for small boats. They get tankers in with oil and provisions so the community can survive so they have two massive pontoons, one of which we're tied up against with a couple of fishing boats.

Colin discovered at the airport that the airline had mislaid his luggage which was not going to arrive until after *Northabout* had sailed. Poor chap had to resort to using gear that I'd left behind!

It's great that Frances is now joining the boat for the trip from Upernavik to Nuuk as she has been responsible for the Polar Ocean Challenge website and for uploading the daily blogs both from myself and various members of the crew.

Upernavik harbour.

Frances Gard, photographer and film maker joined Northabout *on the leg from Upernavik to Nuuk.*

One of Frances' tasks aboard will be to complete a number of video interviews that will go on to form an important record of the voyage. These links and their connection to the Wicked Weather Watch website form the bridge to bringing our message about global warming and environmental change to the wider world, especially to younger people who, after all, are those who will be inheriting the world we leave to them.

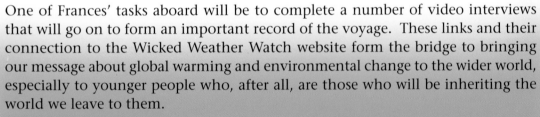

Alison Hallett, an experienced sailor and qualified skipper, sailed on the leg from Upernavik to Nuuk.

Spectacular view from Upernavik airport.

STEVE EDWARDS' BLOG
18 September 2016

As we expected, it was a long night last night as the big swell and northernly winds continued to sweep us along from Upernavik, big surf waves behind us breaking under us. The icebergs were between the size of telly to the size of a house to the size of a grand hotel. They were breaking up, and once or twice right in front of us creating lots a small bergs and ice chunks that don't float so high above the water and so are difficult to spot especially with a large 10 foot swell, they disappear and reappear in the water around us. Another danger with icebergs if you get too close to them is that they can invert, i.e. turn over in the water. We passed a couple that looked like they had already done this and had their 'bottoms up' to us.

The view across a barren Greenland landscape towards Baffin Bay where the drifting ice can be seen – everything from large bergs to small chunks – most of which posed considerable danger to a small boat.

With my absence Steve Edwards and the new skipper, Mike Stewart, will take over the responsibility for uploading the daily ship's log – conditions aboard allowing – a journey which I will follow with great interest (and not a little envy!).

And so, on the afternoon of 17 September, *Northabout* leaves Upernavik heading for her next port of call, Ilulissat, which lies about 500 nautical miles south on the Greenland coast. Those on board are Ros, Steve and Ben Edwards, Frances Gard, Colin Walker, Alison Hallett, Johan and Nikolai, all looking forward to the voyage south, with the forecast set fair for the week-long journey down to Nuuk.

But an unscheduled stiff tailwind pushed *Northabout* along at a brisk 9 knots which, in a choppy sea, made for an uncomfortable few hours for the new arrivals, with Alison, Ros and Frances all being seasick – only Ros of these three being well enough to carry out her watch. With icebergs remaining a constant threat, Mike decided to have three people on watch together, one helming, one at the bow with a powerful torch to spot the bergs, and a standby in the saloon should they be instantly required.

Ben, I think much relieved to have come through all that the North East and North West Passages could throw at him, showed true seamanship by covering for his crewmates and taking on a six-hour straight shift.

With the wind increasing to 25 knots as they neared Ilulissat so the dangers of hitting ice grew and vigilance on the part of those who were fit enough to take their watches became paramount. As I know only too well, the apparent serenity of these huge castles of ice as they sail majestically past can be quite mesmerising, reducing one's sense of just how destructive they can be.

Colin Walker, who oversaw the original refit of Northabout, *joined her again in Upernavik harbour for the voyage to Nuuk.*

Ben sailing down to Ilulissat among the bergs, happy to be away from the rigours of the more extreme passages of the voyage. Greenland was undoubtedly his most enjoyable part of the voyage.

FRANCES GARD'S BLOG
19 September 2016

Night sailing. My watch starts in 4 hours time at 10pm and lasts until 2am. I'm looking forward to it because it should be a clear night by midnight and I think the Aurora is predicted to be strong tonight so I hope it makes an appearance. Alison and Steve are on watch. Ben was asleep but has just risen, in time to get dressed for his watch that starts in 20 mins. Nikolai the captain is also asleep, with his door open to the saloon so he can get up quick when he feels that something has changed in the rhythmic movements of the boat and he may be needed. Which he seems to be very good at.

With visibility falling it was beginning to get tricky seeing the oncoming icebergs against the murky outline of the coast, while the following wind kept *Northabout* clipping along at quite a pace, the genoa up and with the motor on for close-quarters manoeuvring around the ice.

As night fell so this process became even more critical, adding a whole new dimension to playing cat and mouse with the ice, made more difficult by the waves breaking all around, every seething white-top being a possible small berg or partly submerged floe. The darkness was filled with the cry of the bow watch shouting 'go to port, or 'go to starboard', with increasingly urgency, the sweep of their torch flashing back and forth across the blackness of the sea.

As dawn broke the helmsman had a dodgy moment when it was discovered they were heading straight towards a rocky shoal, marked on one of *Northabout*'s charts but not on another – a close shave narrowly averted.

A cheering sun rose as *Northabout* approached Ilulissat harbour which was surrounded by huge jumbles of ice debris. With the benefit of all those hours helming through ice in the North East Passage, Ben steered expertly through the last three miles of very dense ice at slow speed. Entering the harbour they passed by a blood splattered polar bear kill on a floe, but with no bear to be seen.

Northabout, nestled up alongside other boats in Ilulissat harbour.

With a day and a half in port the crew take the opportunity to tidy up the boat and to restock necessary supplies. This done, a party sets off glacier-watching, up to a headland where they can see the ice that feeds into the Jacobshaven fjord and from there out into Baffin Bay – the source of all the icebergs that made getting to Ilulissat such hard work. With the rapidity of the ice melt, the crew were treated to the extraordinary sight of a berg the size of a city park gradually breaking free of the huge ice cliff. Locals say there is much more ice in Ilulissat than 40 years ago because the glaciers are receding and dumping ice even faster into the fjord – the glacier fronts have gone back several miles over that time.

STEVE EDWARDS' BLOG
19 September 2016

Ilulissat has about half as many working dogs as people – about 2,400 dogs (although there were about double that number 20 years ago) all chained firmly to the rocks. They are enthusiastic, strong and friendly but in a slightly dangerous way and are definitely not to be petted. Their puppies are allowed to wander free until five months old and are delightful, if a bit nippy.

The crew at the glacier farm above Jacobshaven fjord.

A spectacular image of the aurora borealis over the Davis Strait.

STEVE EDWARDS' BLOG
21 September 2016

The warm weather and lack of wind has encouraged various crew out of the boat including Nikolai who needed only a T-shirt. The weather has also allowed a few domestic jobs to be carried out, such as doing some washing of tea towels and hanging them out on the jack-stays and genoa sheet to dry. A very domestic looking boat this afternoon.

Back in autumnal England I followed the progress of *Northabout* and her crew down the Greenland coast, wishing I could be with them. This did indeed seem like a most idyllic part of the voyage, with time ashore to relax and explore the extraordinary Greenland landscape and get to meet its people. I was particularly envious of the superb auroras which the crew were enjoying – the photos they posted, though spectacular, never doing justice to the ever-changing mystery of the real thing. Meanwhile, I was busy planning for *Northabout*'s return to Bristol and drumming up media interest in the success of Polar Ocean Challenge.

*   *   *

Despite near zero temperatures, the crew were enjoying some perfect weather as they headed towards Nuuk. On the morning of 21 September *Northabout* once again crossed the Arctic Circle, this time heading south, and this time the crew celebrating with a bottle of Barcardi that Nikolai magicked up from somewhere.

While in this arctic equivalent of the Doldrums, with no wind to speak of and a flat calm sea, Nikolai took the opportunity to service the engine while Ros – small enough to get into the bilges – attempted to reattach the suction pipe for one of the bilge pumps that wasn't working. But without success.

But all good things must end, and I imagine it was with some regret that the crew found themselves fast approaching the harbour at Nuuk towards the end of their Greenland trip and nearing the start point of the Atlantic crossing. Of course not all on board had signed on for the leg back to England and I had been busy making final arrangements for the replacement crew who would be flying out to bring *Northabout* back home.

With Nikolai leaving the boat in Nuuk, *Northabout* would be under the eye of the new skipper, Mike Stewart, with his First Mate, Andrew Coulthurst, my old friend David Wynne Davis, and Rob Hudson. Ben Edwards remains as the only original crew member.

And while all these arrangements are underway, *Northabout* continues her somewhat leisurely way south, eventually arriving at Nuuk just before sunrise on the morning of 22 September, to be greeted on the quayside by Mike.

Here Frances says her goodbyes and catches a flight to Rekyjavik and onwards to home, but not before she and Steve and Ben had rounded up some locals to interview for a video to go on the Wicked Weather Watch website. Ben also got a taste of what 'luxury' sailing might entail when he was invited aboard the yacht *Eagles Quest II*, moored in the harbour.

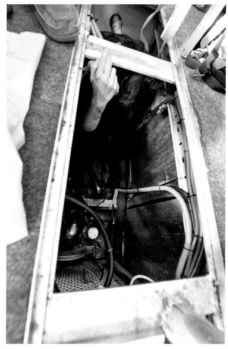

Repairs down in the bilges.

Tiny pinpoints of light greet our arrival in Nuuk at dawn on 22 September.

Eagles Quest II *at anchor in Nuuk.*

Our first day with the new crew. I loved it! David and Rob and I emptied the lazaratte so we could check the auto-helm repair Dad and I had done in Tuktoyuktuk to see if it was still working, and when Mike arrived he had a look and reached the same conclusion. After that we checked the sails and David fixed one of the runners on the mainsail and fixed the guard rail. Andrew tightened the engine mounts that got rid of a very irritating vibration in the table and went though all the basic boat checks you have to do. At one o'clock we said farewell to Eagles Quest *and left the dock. We'd agreed with them we were going to anchor and we gave them our route so they could come and meet us.*

Mike Stewart.

This was an altogether different kind of vessel (a Tayana 58), with her sleek lines and with a greater length than *Northabout,* she did indeed have the appearance of a vessel that might be seen in Monte Carlo rather than Murmansk. A larger boat with a smaller crew certainly appealed to Ben when he was invited aboard by her Hong Kong owner, Kee Duen Chu, who had spent years planning a voyage through the Canadian Arctic to the Mediterranean and had just arrived from Alaska.

Meanwhile, the new skipper of *Northabout* was more interested in his own vessel, anxious to get to know the state of her and her fitness to get himself and his crew safely across the Atlantic. But I had no doubt they were in good hands for Mike, a New Zealander, military trained, had massive experience as a delivery skipper with over 30 000 miles under his belt, on top of his many solo voyages.

On Saturday 24 September, following briefings, repairs to the mainsail, reinforcing a damaged guide-rail with a scrap piece of metal and tightening up the engine mounts *Northabout* sets off for Faeringehavn – a short passage – where Mike's intention is to moor up for the night. The plan on the following day is a little more ambitious: a day sail of perhaps 100 miles. But the weather is favourable, partially sunny with very little wind – the omens are promising!

Rob Hudson.

Faeringehavn is one of the many 'ghost' ports on this vast coastline, haunted by roofless abandoned houses and the hulks of old whaling ships that themselves resemble the skeletal remains of huge sea beasts. Safe inside this anchorage *Eagles Quest II* hoves into sight and her crew join *Northabout*'s for a cuppa.

ROB HUDSONS' BLOG
25 September 2016

The weather is grey, dry and cold, the sea is calm, and there is little wind as we gently cruise down the coast to our next anchorage. Last night was at Faeringehavn, an abandoned Faroese fishing village, in still water surrounded by islands with a few derelict houses on one side. Tonight should be at Fiskenaesset, a fishing village of 230 inhabitants, so it should be a little livelier. So far today we have in 5 hours seen no other living soul. The wildness and solitude is captivating.

Northabout is full of amazing food. In the first two days I've sampled chicken tikka, chicken fricassee, meatballs, chilli, Greenland rollmop herrings (sublime!), Branston pickle, lime and mango chutney, three different types of cheese, Ryvita, cheese crackers, scrambled eggs, tomato soup and endless slices and chunks of fresh brown bread from the onboard breadmaker. This is clearly an expedition that sails on its stomach!!

Northabout tucked into the quiet anchorage at Faeringehavn.

Typical houses in the tiny fishing village of Fiskenaesset with a population of around 250 souls.

Andy Coulthurst, First Mate on the final leg, has sailed extensively in South and Central American waters and in the Pacific. Trained as an environmental consultant, he felt an obvious affinity for the aims of the Polar Ocean Challenge.

The following morning *Northabout* makes for Fiskenaesset, a small fishing settlement some ten hours sailing and, as the weather is good, Mike decides this is a good time for the crew under his command to practice Man Overboard procedures. This involves throwing overboard a bucket tied to the guard rail – this representing the person in the water. Whoever notices cries out 'Man Overboard' to alert the rest of the crew and meanwhile points, and keeps pointing, at the figure in the water so as not to lose sight of them. Everyone on board is assigned a role: helming, control of engine, sending out a mayday call etc., all the time watching (in this case) the bucket bobbing on the surface.

Simply described, *Northabout* is then turned to circle the notional figure in the water, coming round into the wind and, with the engine in neutral, she drifts down on to the 'casualty' securing them with a boat hook or lifeline and guiding them round to the transom to be hauled aboard. Easy enough in calm water but a discipline requiring much skill in heavy seas and well worth running through, as was Mike's simple and sound plan for shortening sail – essential as this might have to be done under pressure, at night, and in marginal conditions. Mike also quickly established his own sea-routine with a two-hourly watch system and with himself or Andy Coulthurst ready to respond. He also established a reefing and stowing procedure prior to stowing the mainsail ready for the ocean voyage.

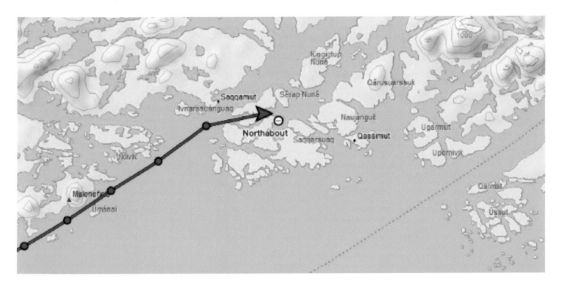

Arriving in the stunningly beautiful anchorage at Ivnarssuangup Nuna.

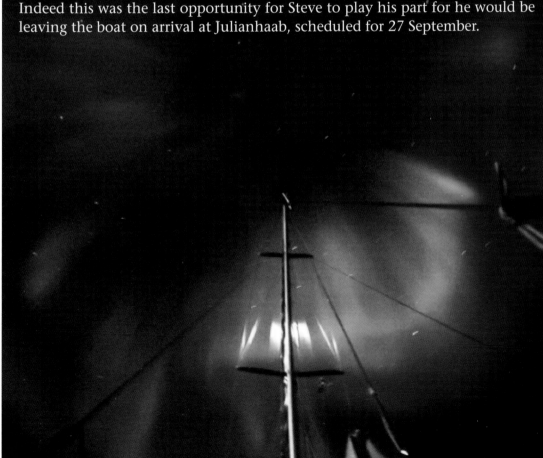

Sensibly, and recognising the greater experience of Ben and Steve aboard *Northabout*, Mike called on them to describe how she performed in various conditions, while he asked Steve to brief the crew on the radar and AIS systems. Indeed this was the last opportunity for Steve to play his part for he would be leaving the boat on arrival at Julianhaab, scheduled for 27 September.

ROB HUDSONS' BLOG
26 September 2016

Many words have been written about the Aurora Borealis or Northern Lights, but none of them do justice to what occurred last night. David WD was on watch from 2000 to 2200, and I was reading in the cabin while everyone else caught up on sleep. About 2130 I looked out the hatch and David said the lights were starting, and I could see curtains forming as I looked out through the deckhouse windows.

Then at 2200 I was at the helm while the heavens danced above me for two glorious hours. Pale green ribbons and curtains stretched from one horizon to the other, twisting and turning, coiling and stretching, and as one spectacle passed another would form ahead. Wow! The lights were bright enough to reflect off the sea, so it was not really dark at all, and Ursa Major was crystal clear behind. No traffic, a couple of lights on the shore as we passed a small settlement. Otherwise just me and the Northern Lights cruising at 6kts down the Greenland coast.

Whales breaching of the coast of Greenland.

Following one more overnight stop in the beautiful anchorage at Ivnarssuangup Nuna, and relishing some best weather of the whole voyage, *Northabout* arrives in Julianehaab. It's obvious from the blogs I've been reading that their voyage down Greenland's west coast has been one of the most life-changing experiences for all on board.

As one last celebratory gesture aboard before flying home, Steve flies the drone off the deck and films *Northabout* anchored up against the austere background of Greenland's many islands.

Northabout *anchored among the islands.*

Julianehaab

Julianehaab – in the native tongue known as Qaqortoq – the crew took the opportunity of the day's layover to prepare themselves and the boat for the challenges of the Atlantic crossing. This included refuelling and replacing one of the batteries that will ensure the chart plotter, navigation lights, interior lighting, electric pumps and bilge pumps don't fail. Most importantly it means that the engine start battery will work when called upon.

Here they meet up again with *Eagles Quest II*. Both south-bound vessels have their eye on the weather ahead which, from the reports, does not look promising. Mike decides to head for Prince Christian Sound, rounding the aptly named Cape Farewell at the southernmost tip of Greenland, which will provide a safe anchorage and an ideal jumping off point once the weather shows signs of improving. Originally he intended to take *Northabout* on an inshore route for this passage but the charts showed too many shallows. There's still plenty of ice offshore, and fog, but this is by far the safest option.

The crew were also delighted to discover that, along with being an excellent skipper, Mike had been a chef in Australia and cooked up a superb feast based on Arctic char.

DAVID WYNNE DAVIS' BLOG
30 September 2016

After a day's layover in Qaqortoq where we replenished and undertook minor repairs, we motor-sailed towards the Southern tip – Cape Farewell. En route we saw more whale spouts, a few seals and a spectacular iceberg. Whilst watching it at close, but safe quarters there was a sharp sound similar to a cannon going off.
Rather than head directly to an anchorage further East, we diverted to Uunartoq a small island famous for its thermal springs. Andrew and I braved the elements in a natural thermal spring which is known to the Norsemen and mentioned in the Sagas. The pool was 30 feet in diameter and 3 foot deep – sharing it with three local children and their shaggy dog! There was a marvellous backdrop of a steep-sided fjord. The water temperature was about 30 degrees and exhilarating.

Northabout *and* Eagles Quest II *sharing the anchorage and the hot springs.*

On 2 October *Northabout,* having rounded Cape Farewell, entered the magnificent Prince Christian Sound on the eastern coast of Greenland from where they expect to set off across the Atlantic the following day, weather permitting. There's significant amounts of ice in the anchorage, scraping on the anchor chain and crunching against the hull.

Mike moves to the easternmost entrance of the sound, close to the weather station at Aappilattoq, a remote fishing village with a population of around a hundred souls. It has a small harbour, more a cleft in the rock, together with a church, about 20 houses, a helipad and radio mast. These are the last people the crew will see as they set off on the final part of their homeward journey.

The weather station at Aappilattoq.

*　　　*　　　*

136

Those of us back in the warmth and safety of our own homes read Mike's blogs of 4–5 October with some alarm at the conditions *Northabout* faced as they entered the North Atlantic – alarm mixed equally with admiration for his calmness in describing the severity of the situation. There's little doubt he was taking into account the effect of his words on the friends and family waiting at home and it's appropriate that I leave him to take up this part of the story in his own words:

Position 59,09.5N   39,18.9W at approx 11.30 UTC 4th October
SHIPSLOG about yesterday and today.
Wind is currently 15KT s.e, baro 986 rising slowly, sea 4m, moderate swell from west, a little current (would be called a sultana in NZ) (eastbound) blue sky and birds everywhere. Sea temp has doubled in 24 hours to 7.7c, air temp 6.7c rising. We have had our angry North Atlantic low blow through during the night, and after our scheduled departure from Greenland, into the western sector of that low, I am very pleased with the vessel and crew's performance in tough conditions. I think the tactic of shakedown and settle in on the vessel, for a week or so, has paid dividends, in as much as no damage, no injury, although there are a few spectacular spits over the side of expensive prepacked food; now fish and Fulmar bait. We have handled the initial blow very well indeed. I am impressed. This sets us up for what may come which could be very much worse as this is; the North Atlantic in Autumn. In fact there is another low that will affect us in the next 24 hours, this will be through by tomorrow midnight, and most of its associated wind is westerly or northerly in

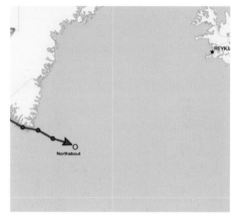

Northabout's *position as she entered the North Atlantic on 4 October.*

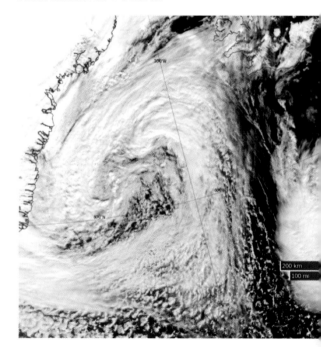

Satellite image of the Atlantic storm.

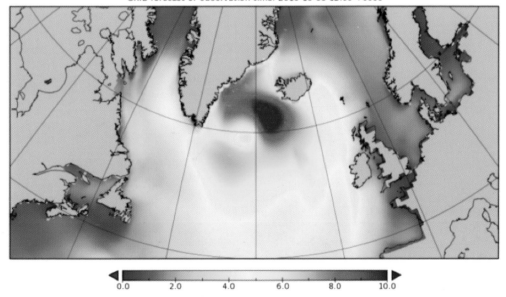

Significant height of combined wind waves and swell
GRIB forecast or observation time: 2016-10-03 12:00 +0000

0.0   2.0   4.0   6.0   8.0   10.0

Imagery of the sea conditions at the start of Northabout's *Atlantic crossing.*

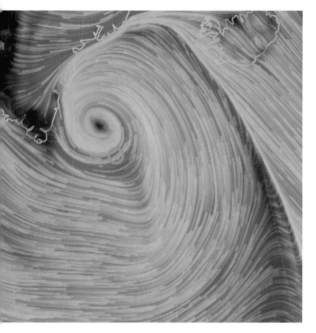

Not an abstract painting but the eye of the storm off the Greenland coast.

our bit, anyway we take what we get here, its as simple as that. We have handled this at 50 KT with around 7m seas, (occasionally 8-9m) so our confidence levels are good. I heaved the boat to for a few minutes to test how she behaved, and she was 'OK' sitting duck like as the rollers powered through beneath us. During the evening, we were hit by one breaker, as always, there's a set bigger than the rest, and of course one broke over the boat, we were lifted and pushed sideways like a cork, but did not go over to any degree, which says volumes for our stability curve. The longer range predictions are good for our run to Ireland. We could have waited in Greenland, but as we only do 6 knots, and our ETA is in around 7 days, sooner or later we would have had to deal with rough weather, it has now been done while we are fresh, and well fed, and alert. Well done to NORTHABOUT, a tough old girl, and Crew, especially 'Youngest' Ben, who deserves a skippers 'mention in dispatches', at least, for 'steadiness under pressure on watch' and remaining on deck when required. He also went forward in big seas, to fix an issue with the main halyard without question, was safe the whole time and sorted out the job smartly and professionally as I expected of this talented lad. Well done Ben our youngest. Also well done to Andrew the Mate, chef David, our Dad and tomato soup specialist, and Uncle Rob who is keeping us going with hot brews and Marmite (I wish it was Vegemite).

Position, 58.10.1N 35,37.2W wind 25 kt, gusting 35 kt, sea moderate to rough, blue sky and birds. temp 17.7c, water 8.1c, SOG 8.5 kt, CSE 113T, DTW (Bantry Bay) 952 nm BARO 974 rising. 5 Oct 11.30 UTC

We have progressed through our second 'low' without mishap, in fact we managed to stay in a small area around 60 miles wide of relatively light winds showing green and blue on the Grib file. Green is good, Blue is Paradise, Dark Magenta is something I would rather not experience, thanks. In our patch of tranquility, for which I will take full but undue credit for manoeuvring us into, we could feel the swell and waves generated by the gale force winds (showing 63 KT gusts on the weather map – tinge of Magenta) around us to the north and west. Now after 48 hours of tumbling around and hanging on, I reckon we are through the most difficult part. After a weather analysis this morning it looks very good for our run to Bantry Bay, and a Guinness, staying in a southern sector of a low in our way which should give us following winds, it makes all the difference. Crew and boat are well. Everyone is sporting a Shackleton/Mawson style beard depending on your personal hero, and we are all looking distinctly British and (Kiwi) 'Salty Sea Dog'. Ben included, Zorro style whisps on the chin, a good effort at 14, going on 15.

The scene from my dark bunk one eye open to feign sleep, around 3 AM yesterday: Retching, twice, followed by a final sustained, retch in a much higher pitch, and then toilet pumping like billy-oh... someone peers into my cabin, unidentified, just making sure I'm still on board I would think, satisfied I'm actually there, he disappears forward, it remains a mystery who it was. WHUMP! a hard hitting wall of a water knocks us firmly sideways, then the vertigo of 26 tons shifting sideways and downwards about 30 feet, roll and recovery and water washing everywhere decks, widows, cockpit, someone has a fire hose spraying on us, a few clangs and clatters as she comes up, settles and powers ahead after a serious knock. I get up slide the hatch and see a dripping helmsman, water inches deep at his feet, wet streams from his peak and face is soaking, and get a solid thumbs up, you ok? I shout... another thumbs up, shake my head, we laugh together, and I'm back below. You could easily believe there was a gang of burly angry construction workers with sledges and picks bashing on the hull trying to get in at us. Noise and motion, for 16 hours.

Dawn breaks, some blue patches, and birds everywhere, the sea uniform grey, although she still looks a bit angry with the odd hill-size roller lurking around. A brew is on, McVities Chocolate Digestives, life sustaining, are ready, and the day begins. 5 days to Bantry Bay and under us, around 2 miles down is the bottom. I won't go into what may be down there!

MIKE STEWART'S BLOG
9 October 2016

Firstly an apology for missing daily logs, we have had our hands full keeping the boat moving SE against persistent headwinds and squally conditions.

From leaving the intense low systems of greenland the weather has steadily moved towards a pattern of wet, windy, relatively warm lows, overtaking us from behind, producing squalls, some as strong as 50 KT estimated, for a short period. This has meant constant attention to sail plan, engine revs and lookout. The latter being all the more important as we have seen two vessels directly in our track, both picked up on ever working radar and mark one eyeball. A large Japanese trawler and a 128m tanker both heading north. Well done watch lookouts.

My crew are content, the vessel is performing well, and we are all hanging in there after a challenging 5 days, We are steadily plowing a sea-furrow east, south east and east again...

ETA Dingle in two days with a good bit of Irish luck for this an Irish flagged vessel.

Which way now? Having brought her through the worst of the storm, Mike plots Northabout's *next waypoint on the voyage home.*

Having weathered the storm the crew then suffer the frustration of constant headwinds that hamper forward progress and have Mike taking down all sails and re-sorting to the engine. From leaving the intense low systems off Greenland the weather steadily moved towards a pattern of wet, windy, relatively warm lows, overtaking *Northabout* from behind, and producing squalls, some as strong as 50 knot estimated, for short periods. This meant constant attention to the sail plan, engine revs and lookout – and unspoken frustration among the crew who just want to get home.

Between the 5–10th October the headwinds continue to hold the boat away from the Irish coast, their initial landing point before taking the boat onward to Bristol. I know just how frustrating it can be, bashing on through days of headwinds, putting up with the incessant engine noise, vibrations, sails flogging, lines banging and a general hobby-horse motion of the boat, as she beats to windward through the oncoming waves. But, eventually, ten days after leaving Greenland a feint smudge of darker grey appears off *Northabout*'s port bow – land ho! Ireland!

Almost as though drawn by some mystic Celtic compass, *Northabout* heads not for her intended landfall in Ireland but, by dint of all those headwinds, fetches up a stone's throw from her home port, the very place where Jarlath Cunnane first laid her keel.

After several days of constant use and misuse the heads finally get a tidy up.

Andy catches up on some rest between watches as Northabout *edges towards the Irish coast.*

Heading into the morning sun and towards the coast of Ireland.

Celebration in County Mayo with Jarlath and the crew of Northabout.

Tying up beside the Blacksod Bay fishing boats undoubtedly brought immediate relief to Mike and his crew – but mixed emotions too, as are often felt went challenges are overcome, goals achieved. Not least for Ben, who had completed the whole voyage, for this journey signalled the end of a major waypoint in his life.

An emotional moment too for Jarlath and his the Irish crew who turned up to greet their old vessel and who promptly took the new arrivals to the local hostelry for a few pints and a traditional Irish sing-song. Frances Gard turned up out of the blue, never one to miss such an occasion.

The following day *Northabout* sailed for Westport with Jarlath on board, returning to the place he had built her in 2001. It was a poignant moment with RTE News and several journalists present to record the event. Here the crew once again celebrated, with unprecedented hospitality shown by their Irish hosts, with many toasts to all those involved in the Polar Ocean Challenge, and to *Northabout* whose expedition log recorded a total distance travelled of 10 400 nautical miles since leaving Bristol on 19 June.

With Andy leaving the boat in Westport, on 14 October *Northabout* sets sail for Dingle, where Steve rejoins her and helps with a little refurbishment before sailing with her back to Portishead. It was as though the old girl knew she was on the final stretch for, with the aid of a following wind, she perfectly galloped along with the bit between her teeth, reaching a spirited 15 knots at one point.

MIKE STEWART'S BLOG
12 October 2016

So Anyway, by nightfall we were tied up along some very businesslike Blacksod Bay fishing trawlers, and our reception party, a local team of enthusiasts, led by Mr Jarlath Cunnane, Northabout's *builder, were there to meet us, all previous crew interested and supportive of our expedition. The lighthouse keeper was even there to take line, God Bless him. We like Lighthouses.*

As I write we are heading into Northabout's *registered home port, Westport. I don't know about inanimate objects possessing souls, although I would think any self-respecting Inuit, or Maori for that matter, will tell you its a natural state of affairs, but I think this old boat wanted to go home one last time, and organised the weather around it! We will be alongside in an hour. We and probably* Northabout *too are really looking forward to it.*

As many of those who could, took part in the homecoming celebrations in front of the media on board Northabout *in Bristol.*

*   *   *

I was standing on the lock at Portishead to greet *Northabout*'s return when she hove into view, her crew waving frantically as they approached. I knew that everyone on board, in fact everyone who'd played a part in making the Polar Ocean Challenge such a marvellous and successful project, would be experiencing their own feelings at this moment. For myself, the moment represented the culmination of years of hard work, and if I felt a sense of pride it was in having grown this project from the seed of an idea into something that was far more than the sum of its parts – a vision, the fruits of which I hoped would extend beyond this moment and play a small part in bringing about the changes that are necessary to help understand and counter the effects of global warming.

As Mike Stewart graciously handed back command of *Northabout*, I took her once again along the Bristol Channel, under Brunel's magnificent bridge, to her original berth alongside the SS *Great Britain*. It felt like home.

THE GOLDEN JOURNEY TO SAMARKAND

We who with songs beguile your pilgrimage
And swear that Beauty lives though lilies die,
We Poets of the proud old lineage
Who sing to find your hearts, we know not why, -

What shall we tell you? Tales, marvellous tales
Of ships and stars and isles where good men rest,
Where nevermore the rose of sunset pales,
And winds and shadows fall towards the West:

And there the world's first huge white-bearded kings
In dim glades sleeping, murmur in their sleep,
And closer round their breasts the ivy clings,
Cutting its pathway slow and red and deep.

And how beguile you? Death has no repose
Warmer and deeper than the Orient sand
Which hides the beauty and bright faith of those
Who make the Golden Journey to Samarkand.

And now they wait and whiten peaceably,
Those conquerors, those poets, those so fair:
They know time comes, not only you and I,
But the whole world shall whiten, here or there;

When those long caravans that cross the plain
With dauntless feet and sound of silver bells
Put forth no more for glory or for gain,
Take no more solace from the palm-girt wells.

When the great markets by the sea shut fast
All that calm Sunday that goes on and on:
When even lovers find their peace at last,
And Earth is but a star, that once had shone.

James Elroy Flecker